Carson-Dellosa Publishing

Supports
The Four-Blocks®
Literacy Model

Assessment and Intervention for Struggling Readers

by

Karen Loman

Editor
Joey Bland

Cover Design
Jennifer Collins

This book is dedicated to my husband, Chris, who saw me as an author long before I did. Thank you for believing in me and encouraging me to do more than I ever imagined.

I would also like to thank:

Dr. Barbara Condra for giving me an opportunity to share my passion for, and knowledge of, reading with the Title One Reading program at Eastwood Hills Elementary in Raytown, Missouri. Thank you!

Dr. Dorothy Hall for her unique ability to make the Blocks come alive. Dottie, like my husband, encouraged me to write. Your encouragement and support have made the development of this book a joy.

ISBN 0-88724-784-9

Foreword

Often after Pat Cunningham or I finish a workshop on the Four Blocks, someone will come up to us and say, "I really like the idea of doing Four Blocks in the classroom but I am a *special* teacher and do not have a class or group for two hours. How can I do the Four Blocks in the amount of time I have?" The truth is you can't! What these teachers or specialists can do is some of the activities that their children need and that they aren't getting in their classrooms. Or, they can assess them and choose the activities their students need more help with. Karen Loman did this as a Title One Reading specialist in her school. I encouraged her to write this book to tell others how she did this.

In *Assessment and Intervention for Struggling Readers*, Karen tells teachers how they can use and adapt many of the Four-Blocks strategies for either classroom use when students need extra help, or how a special teacher can do this for a student or groups of students. Schools and school systems that use non-certified instructors to help their struggling students will find this a valuable tool also.

Dorothy P. Hall

Table of Contents

Table of Contents

Introduction

Welcome to *Assessment and Intervention for Struggling Readers*. This book is intended to assist classroom teachers, Title One teachers, teaching aides or associates, tutors, and other adults that work with children experiencing reading difficulty. These adults will find *Assessment and Intervention for Struggling Readers* a complete resource for identifying student needs and providing specific strategies that will accelerate student learning.

Here are a few examples of how *Assessment and Intervention for Struggling Readers* might be used to assist students.

- Classroom teachers may use *Assessment and Intervention for Struggling Readers* with small groups of children needing additional assistance.

  Jay is a first grade student at Central Elementary. His teacher, Mrs. Smith, has identified Jay as needing extra assistance. Each morning Jay participates in a two-hour communication arts block with his classmates. His teacher is using the Four-Blocks® Literacy Model (Cunningham, Hall, and Sigmon, 1999). Students in Jay's class have guided reading, self-selected reading, writing, and time for working with words every day. After the communication arts block students participate in literacy centers for 30 minutes. Three days a week, Jay and other students needing acceleration strategies work with the teacher during this time. The first thing Mrs. Smith did was assess Jay's current skills and strategies. She found that Jay needs to work on phonemic awareness and letters and sounds. The teachers at Central Elementary have leveled all of their student reading materials with *Matching Books to Readers: Using Leveled Books in Guided Reading, K-3* (Fountas and Pinnell, 1999), so they can more accurately assign Guided Reading and Self-Selected Reading books to children. Mrs. Smith selects books at level C for Jay's small group to read. Each day she has the group read a book, practice letters and sounds, high-frequency words on their portable word walls, and blending and segmenting words.

  In January Mrs. Smith reassesses all of her students. Jay now knows all of the letters and sounds and is reading independently at level E. Jay has made more progress than some of the other students in his group, so Mrs. Smith has Jay begin meeting with another group. His new group meets the other two days of the week. This group reads and writes daily. Jay really likes writing. He is making a list of things he would like for his birthday.

- Title One teaching aides or associates may use *Assessment and Intervention for Struggling Readers* with small groups of students. These groups may be push-in or pullout. A push-in group is directed by a teacher or associate who goes into a classroom and works with a group in the context of the classroom. A pull-out group leaves the classroom to work together with a teacher or associate.

  Jay's third grade sister, Britany, has also been identified as needing extra assistance. Britany "reads" quite well but has trouble understanding what she reads. Students in her class complete a 20-minute daily review activity before the communication arts block begins. Britany's teacher, Mrs. Davis, has Britany and two other students spend that time with a Title One teaching associate, Ms. Carlson. Ms. Carlson has completed a reading profile to determine each student's reading strengths and weaknesses. She groups the children she works with so she can focus on specific reading levels and strategies. She selects level K books for Britany's group to read. They spend most of their group time reading and discussing the story. They are starting a new book today, *Wagon Wheels* by Barbara Brenner. Ms. Carlson asks the students to guess what is going to happen in their new story. Then, she teaches them important vocabulary words they are going to see. She introduces the story to them by reading the first chapter to them and thinking aloud as the group thinks along. Britany enjoys hearing Ms. Carlson think aloud, especially when she talks about things that take place in the book that also happened to her. After hearing the chapter, students will reread it with Ms. Carlson. They will finish today's session by talking about what happened in the first chapter, checking their predictions, and making new predictions.

- Tutors will find *Assessment and Intervention for Struggling Readers* a valuable resource as they develop lessons and activities.

  Several students at Central Elementary qualify for tutoring before or after school. Tutoring teams meet for 45 minutes twice a week. All students must have reading profiles completed before tutoring begins. Mr. Jacobs, the PE teacher, is one of the tutors. The profiles he has completed on Jim, Juan, and Bailee help him plan for his group. He knows that the three second graders are reading at level G. He has access to many leveled books and plans to get *More Spaghetti I Say* by Rita Golden Gelman for them to read at their first session. He also plans to give everyone their own portable word wall folder so they can keep track of the new words they learn each week. Today, they will clap the new word wall words and play Be a Mind Reader. He will use a Guess the Covered Word lesson to teach three reading strategies that will help Jim, Juan, and Bailee. Then he will introduce *More Spaghetti I Say* by echo reading it with students.

Chapter One

Assessment

It is often easy to identify the children in our classrooms experiencing reading difficulties. Most often their reading is labored and deliberate, they have a small sight vocabulary, and struggle when reading new words. Some children who are having trouble are more difficult to identify. They are able to "read" all of the words; however, they don't apply meaning to what they have read. Before we can assist our struggling readers we must first determine who needs additional assistance, then we must decide what kind of assistance would be most helpful. Both of these concerns may be addressed by using informal assessment tools. The completed assessments will be used to create a reading profile. The reading profile will guide how groups will be formed, what strategies will be taught, and how often groups will meet.

It will be necessary to use a wide range of assessments to accurately assess each child's current skill level. For young children it will be important to know what they already understand about print and the English language. These are often called Measures of Emergent Literacy. Measures of Emergent Literacy assess:

- print concepts,
- phonemic awareness, and
- letter name and sound identification.

Assessments that measure print concepts assess what the child knows about books (Clay, 1985). Does she know the cover of the book? Does she know to read from left to right? Can she identify a word? Can she follow along? These are important concepts that must be developed before she can be a successful reader.

Phonemes are the smallest units of sound that matter in language. Phonemic awareness is the ability to hear the parts of words, separate the parts, put them back together, and then change them to make new words (Adams, 1990). Phonemic awareness has been shown to be an indicator of reading success (Snow, Burns, and Griffin, 1998). The more students play with words orally, the more successful they will be reading them.

And finally, what do students know about the English alphabet? It is important that they can name the letters of the alphabet and then associate a sound to that letter.

Students who are successful with Measures of Emergent Literacy should be assessed to determine how well they can read, which includes decoding and comprehension. The tools used to assess this are called running records (Clay, 1993) and informal reading inventories. The informal reading inventory is designed to determine a child's reading level, specific strengths and weaknesses in word recognition, and ability to read with comprehension. This is determined by analyzing the student's correct and incorrect responses that are recorded by the instructor as students read orally. Informal reading inventories are given occasionally, generally at the beginning and end of the year.

Benchmark books may also be used as a placement tool to determine a child's independent and instructional reading levels. Children are given a benchmark book, a book at a specific reading level, and their oral reading is recorded. Several companies sell benchmark books. The Wright Group and Rigby Company have benchmark books available. The *Developmental Reading Assessment* (Celebration Press, 1997) may also be used as a benchmarking tool. The DRA is a series of individual stories that have been leveled from A to 44. Students read the selections and answer comprehension questions to determine appropriate reading levels.

Ongoing assessments are important to determine how well students are progressing. These assessments are called running records. Students read orally as the instructor takes a running record of what the student says. The student's correct and incorrect responses are recorded and analyzed to determine what the student understands and what she needs to practice.

Included in *Assessment and Intervention for Struggling Readers* are assessments for print concepts, phonemic awareness, letters and sounds, and running records. It will be necessary to purchase an informal reading inventory for students reading beyond grade one. You may also want to consider purchasing a set of benchmark books as placement tools.

There are many informal reading inventories available for purchase. When selecting an informal reading inventory look at the grade levels addressed, how sight words are assessed, the types of literature included, and how comprehension is assessed. Choose an inventory that begins at grade one and assesses at one or two grade levels beyond the age of the students you are working with. For example, if you are working with students in kindergarten to grade five, you will want an assessment that assesses grades one to six or grades one to seven. Sight words may be assessed in a list form or in a sentence (context). If there is a choice, sight words will be best assessed in context. This allows you an opportunity to determine how well students know individual words and how well they utilize context cues.

Students may be assessed multiple times over the course of a year. Informal reading inventories that have different pieces of literature at each level ensures that students are not rereading familiar stories. It will also be helpful to assess students reading narrative text (fiction) and expository text (nonfiction). Finally, the comprehension measure should include simple, factual questions as well as more complex inferential questions to determine how well the student recalls what was read.

Three reading inventories you might want to look at are:

- Basic Reading Inventory: Pre-Primer through Grade Twelve & Early Literacy Assessments by Jerry Johns (1997)
- The Stieglitz Informal Reading Inventory: Assessing Reading Behaviors from Emergent to Advanced Levels by Ezra L. Stieglitz and Virginia Lanigan (1997)
- Developmental Reading Assessment by Joetta Beaver (1997)

The following pages include:

- which assessments to give if you are identifying emergent readers or assessing readers,
- directions on how to give each assessment,
- a copy of each assessment form(s),
- a place to record results for multiple students, and
- a description of how to analyze the information on the assessment tool.

Identifying Emergent Readers

Assessing emergent readers:

- What does the student know about print? Does she understand how books work? Does she know that reading happens from left to right?

  Administer Print Concepts Assessment on page 12.

- What does she know about sounds? Can she distinguish one sound from another? Can she isolate the sounds in a word? Can she identify rhyming words?

  Administer Phonemic Awareness Assessment on pages 18-19.

- Can she name the letters of the alphabet and their sounds?

  Administer Letters and Sounds Assessment on pages 23-24.

Administering the Assessment: Print Concepts

Students that have been read to as young children come to school with many print concepts. They understand that the cover of the book tells what the story is about. They know that the pages turn from right to left and that the print is read from left to right and top to bottom. If students have not had many reading experiences they may be missing some of this critical information (Clay, 1985). To determine what students understand about printed materials administer the Print Concepts Assessment.

To conduct this assessment you will need a copy of page 12 and a copy of a short picture book. This book will be read with students as a model. The book you choose should have a single line of text on each page, a clear story line, and NOT be familiar to students. Books such as *Whose Mouse Are You?* by Robert Kraus, *Titch* by Pat Hutchins, or *Mrs. Wishy-Washy* by Joy Cowley are examples of books that meet the criteria.

1. Begin by handing the book to the child upside down, spine first and say, "Show me the front of the book." Put a ✓ if the child turns the book around correctly, put a – if they do not.
2. Read the title of the book and ask, "What do you think this book is about?" Write down what the student says. Put a ✓ if the child's answer is appropriate, put a – if it is not. Note: The response does not need to be correct to be appropriate.
3. Now say, "I would like to begin reading the story, but I need your help. Please open the book and point to where I should begin reading." Put a ✓ if the child points to the first word, put a – if he does not.
4. Now say, "Which way do I go while I'm reading?" Put a ✓ if the child's points or says right, put a – if he does not.
5. Now say, "What do you do while I am reading to you?" Put a ✓ if the child's answer is appropriate, put a – if it is not.

6. Read the first page and say, "What should I do now?" Put a ✓ if the child says or shows that you should turn the page, put a – if he does not.
7. Read the first page you turned to but not the facing page and say, "Point to where I go next." Put a ✓ if the child's points or says the page on the right, put a – if he does not.
8. Read until the middle of the text. Use two pages to ask:
   - "Point to one letter." Put a ✓ if the child points to one letter, put a – if he does not.
   - "Point to one word." Put a ✓ if the child points to one word, put a – if he does not.
   - You point to the capital H and say, "Point to a letter that is like this one." Put a ✓ if the child points to the lowercase h, put a – if he does not.
9. Turn the page and say, "Let's read these pages together. I'll read and you point." Finish reading the book. Put a ✓ if the child touches each word as you read it, put a – if he does not.
10. Now ask, "What was this story about?" Write down what the student says. Put a ✓ if the child's answer is appropriate, put a – if it is not.
11. Tell the child you are going to reread some of the sentences from the story and you want him to let you know if they make sense or not. Select five sentences to read. Scramble three of them so they no longer make sense. Put a ✓ if the child's answer is appropriate, put a – if it is not.

Print Concepts Assessment

Student Name	Date	✓ for correct answer – for incorrect answer Write student responses when appropriate.

Used with the book:	✓ / –	Print Concept
1. Hand the book to the child upside down, spine first and say, "Show me the front of the book."		book layout
2. Read the title of the book and ask, "What do you think this book is about?"		comprehension: prediction
3. "I would like to begin reading the story, but I need your help. Please open the book and point to where I should begin reading."		directionality: where to begin
4. "Which way do I go while I'm reading?"		directionality: left to right
5. "What do you do while I am reading to you?"		listens attentively
6. Read the first page and say, "What should I do now?"		directionality: turn page
7. Read the second page, but not the facing page, and say, "Point to where I go next."		directionality: left to right
8. Read until the middle of the text. Use two pages and say:		terminology:
a. "Point to one letter."		letter
b. "Point to one word."		word
c. Point to the capital _____. "Point to a letter that is like this one."		matching
9. Turn the page and say, "Let's read these pages together. I'll read and you point." Finish reading the book.		speech to match print
10. "What was this story about?"		comprehension: summarization
11. Tell the child you are going to reread some of the sentences and you want him or her to let you know if it makes sense or not.		comprehension: text meaning
a. ______________________________.		
b. ______________________________.		
c. ______________________________.		
d. ______________________________.		
e. ______________________________.		

Print Concepts Summary

Teacher | Date | ✓ for correct answer – for incorrect answer

Student Name	book layout	predict	begin on left	left to right	listens	turns page	letter	word	match letters	match speech to print	summary	text meaning

Analyzing the Results: Print Concepts

Record student responses in each column of the Print Concepts Summary. When there is more than one choice (such as question 8 and 11), put a ✓ if 80% of the answers are correct, put a – if less than 80% of the answers are correct. For example, if the student can identify four of the five mixed-up sentences correctly, then put a ✓ on the summary form. If she can identify four of the five mixed-up sentences correctly then put a ✓ on the summary. If she identifies less than four of them correctly, place a –.

Once all of the students' responses have been recorded use a highlighting marker to highlight all of the incorrect responses. These are the skills that are identified as inaccurate or undeveloped. Once all of the skills are highlighted, look at the students that need assistance. Students with similar needs should come together as a group to work on learning about that print concept. These groups should be flexible. Once a student is able to demonstrate the skill, she should no longer be a member of the group.

There are suggested activities in Chapter Two that address learning print concepts. One of the most important activities for promoting print concepts is reading to and with children and discussing the print concept they don't yet understand.

Administering the Assessment: Phonemic Awareness

Phonemic awareness is the ability to hear the order of spoken sounds (Snow, Burns, and Griffin, 1998). A child's level of phonemic awareness is correlated to their reading success. Playing with the sounds within words helps develop phonemic awareness. This is done orally without any printed words or sentences.

Some students need direct instruction in hearing the sounds within words. An assessment of the child's level of phonemic awareness will tell us if he needs help and if so, with what stage. For more information on the stages of phonemic awareness see Chapter Four.

To conduct this assessment you will need six counters (any penny-shaped object) for children to manipulate and one copy each of pages 18-19.

1. Begin by saying, "I will push one counter at a time as I say some words. You will point to the counters that show two words that are the same." You push one counter at a time toward the child as you say each of the following words:

   dan - dan - den

   puck - ruck - puck

   tiff - kit - kit

   been - band - been

   cot - cot - bet

   Put a ✓ if the child's answer is correct, put a – if it is not.
2. Now say, "Do these words begin with the same sound?"

   leg - lunch

   duck - pan

   sun - moon

   fork - fish

   chocolate - cheese

   Put a ✓ if the child's answer is correct, put a – if it is not.
3. Now say, "How many words are in this sentence?" Have children move the counters as you say each word.

   I like dogs.

   What is your favorite color?

   This movie is good.

   I live in a green house.

   Do you have a pet?

   Put a ✓ if the child's answer is correct, put a – if it is not.

4. Now say, "Do you know any words that rhyme?" List any rhyming words the child says. Then say, "Do these words rhyme?"

   cat - hat

   say - way

   please - play

   like - bike

   dog - door

   Put a ✓ if the child's answer is correct, put a – if it is not.

5. Then say, "Tell me a word that rhymes with this word."

   we

   shop

   take

   that

   bike

   Write the word the child says. Then put a ✓ if the word rhymes, put a – if it does not.

6. Now say, "We can tell how many parts are in a word by clapping as we say the word. Let's do your name first." Say the child's name, clapping the syllables as you say it. Then, practice the following words with the child:

   table

   chair

   window

   Now have the child say and clap the words on her own. When she is done ask her how many times she clapped. Record what she says.

   here

   up

   children

   pencil

   come

   and

   another

   went

   little

   bicycle

   Put a ✓ if the number is correct, put a – if it is not.

7. Now say, "How many sounds do you hear in these words?" Have children use the counters if needed.

   dog (3)

   go (2)

   cat (3)

   I (1)

   tea (2)

   Record thc number the child says. Put a ✓ if the number is correct, put a – if it is not.

8. Now say, "I am going to say the sounds in some words. When I am done you tell me what the word is. Let's do some practice words together first." Practice the following words with the child:

   f - i - sh

   n - o - d

   p - e - t

   Tell the child it is their turn to do it by themselves.

   h - a - t

   s - i - p

   d - o - t

   b - e - d

   g - u - m

   Write the word the child says. Put a ✓ if the word is correct, put a – if it is not.

9. Finally say, "I am going to say a word. You tell me all of the sounds in the word." Do some practice words if the child does not understand.

   big

   map

   cut

   meet

   goat

   Write the sounds the child says with a – between sounds (e.g., b-i-g). Put a ✓ if the sounds are correct, put a – if it they are not.

Phonemic Awareness Assessment

Student Name	Recorder	Date	✓ for correct answer – for incorrect answer

Can identify which words are the same:		Can identify same beginning sound:			
You say: Point to the counters that show two words that are the same.	✓ / –	You say: Do these words begin with the same sound?	✓ / –	You say: How many words are in this sentence? (use counters)	✓ / –
dan - dan - den		leg - lunch		I like dogs.	
puck - ruck - puck		duck - pan		What is your favorite color?	
tiff - kit - kit		sun - moon		This movie is good.	
been - band - been		fork - fish		I live in a green house	
cot - cot - bet		chocolate - cheese		Do you have a pet?	

Notes

Can identify rhyming words:			Can supply rhyming words:		
You say: Do you know any words that rhyme? (list below)	You say: Do these words rhyme?	✓ / –	You say: Tell me a word that rhymes with this word.	Student Response	✓ / –
	cat- hat		we		
	say - way		shop		
	please - play		take		
	like - bike		that		
	dog - door		bike		

Notes

Phonemic Awareness Assessment-Part 2

Can identify number of syllables in words:

You say: We can tell how many parts in a word by clapping as we say the word. Let's do your name first.	You say:	✓ / –	You say:	✓ / –
Practice words (clap together)	here		and	
student's name	up		another	
table	children		went	
chair	pencil		little	
window	come		bicycle	

Notes

Can identify the number of sounds in a word:

You say: How many sounds do you hear in these words?		✓ / –
dog	(3)	
go	(2)	
cat	(3)	
I	(1)	
tea	(2)	

Can blend parts of a word into its whole:

You say: Say these sounds.	Student Response	✓ / –
h - a - t		
s - i - p		
d - o - t		
b - e - d		
g - u - m		

Can segment words into parts:

You say: Which sounds do you hear?	Student Response	✓ / –
big		
map		
cut		
meet		
goat		

Notes

Phonemic Awareness/Letters and Sounds Summary

Teacher | Date | ✓ for correct answer – for incorrect answer

Student Name	Phonemic Awareness									Letter Identification		
	identify same word	identify same beginning sounds	identify # of words in sentence	identify rhyming words	supply rhyming words	identify # of syllables	identify # of sounds in a word	blends sounds	segments sounds	name /54	sound /54	word /54

Analyzing the Results: Phonemic Awareness

Record student responses in each column of the Phonemic Awareness/Letters and Sounds Summary. Put a ✓ if 80% of the answers are correct (four out of five); put a – if less than 80% of the answers are correct.

Once all of the students' responses have been recorded, use a highlighting marker to highlight all of the – marks. These indicate the skills that are identified as inaccurate or undeveloped. Once all of the skills are highlighted, look at the students that need assistance. Students with similar needs should come together as a group to work on learning about that print concept. These groups should be flexible. Once a student is able to demonstrate the skill, she should no longer be a member of the group.

There are suggested activities in Chapter Three to address learning about phonemic awareness. All of them require working with counters and pictures, without any printed words or materials. It is important to separate print from sounds. Once print has been added to the activity it becomes a phonics activity, not a phonemic awareness activity.

Administering the Assessment: Letters and Sounds

Children that can identify the names and sounds of the letters of the alphabet have a foundation that will help them as they later learn sight words and how to decode new words (Snow, Burns, and Griffin, 1998). A child's level of letter and sound learning is correlated to their reading success.

Some students need direct instruction in learning the names and sounds of the letters of the alphabet. An assessment of the child's letter knowledge will tell us what letters and sounds she knows and what letters and sounds will need to be practiced. This allows the practice time to be very targeted and brief.

The assessment, adapted from Clay's Observation Survey (1993), will ask students to identify the name of the letter, the beginning sound of the letter, and any word they know that begins with that sound. Many children will be able to identify a word that begins with the correct sound before they can isolate the beginning sound.

Make a copy of page 24. Create a "window" for viewing each letter by cutting a piece of tag board to 11" x 4". Then cut a small square (1" x $\frac{1}{2}$") out of the rectangle about a quarter of the way from the top. This will allow the child to see only one letter at a time.

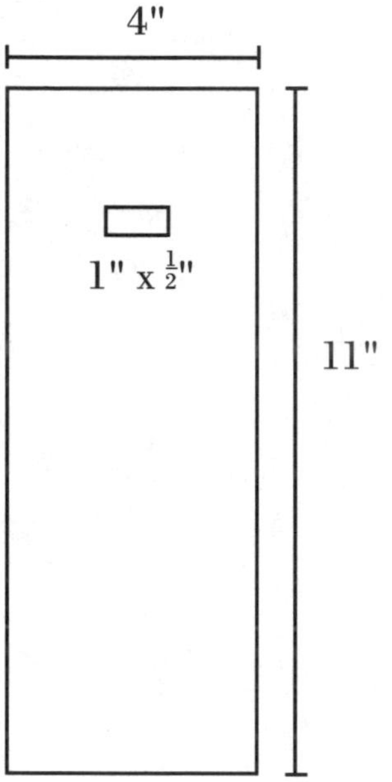

Place the copy of page 24 in front of the child. Place the "window" over the first letter. You will need a copy of page 23 to record what each child says.

1. Ask the child to tell you the name of the letter. Place a ✓ in the box if the letter name is correct. If the child gives an incorrect letter name, write the name of the letter he says.
2. Now ask the child to tell you the sound of that letter. Place a ✓ in the box if the letter sound is correct. If it is a vowel sound, correct or incorrect, indicate if it is the short sound (ă) or the long sound (ā). If the child gives an incorrect letter sound, write the sound that they say by writing it between //. For example, if the letter is c and the sound given was "wuh" it would be written /w/.
3. Finally, ask the child to tell you a word that begins with that sound. Write the word in the box under "word" if the word begins with that sound. If the child gives an incorrect word, write the word in the last column "incorrect word."
4. Move the window across the page (left to right) for the child to read the next letter.

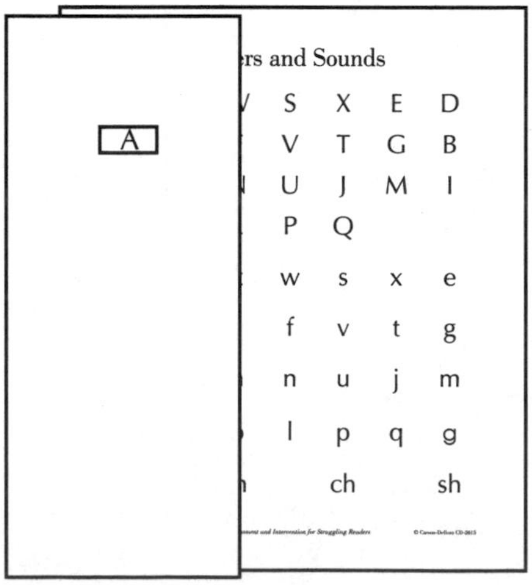

Letters and Sounds Assessment

Date ___________ Student Name ______________________ Grade ____ Recorder ______________

	Letter Name	Letter Sound	Word	Incorrect Word		Letter Name	Letter Sound	Word	Incorrect Word
					ɑ				
C					c				
Z					z				
W					w				
S					s				
X					x				
E					e				
D					d				
A					a				
R					r				
F					f				
V					v				
T					t				
G					g				
B					b				
Y					y				
H					h				
N					n				
U					u				
J					j				
M					m				
I					i				
K					k				
O					o				
L					l				
P					p				
Q					q				
					ɡ				
Total	26	26	26			28	28	28	
wh					ch				
th					sh				

Unknown Letters (list below)

Unknown Sounds (mark as / /)

Marking Responses

Letter Names

Correct Response ✓
Incorrect Response / /

Letter Sounds

Correct Response ✓
Incorrect Response / /
Vowel Sound (ă ā)

Word

Record words in the appropriate column.

Adapted from An Observation Survey of Early Literacy Achievement by Marie Clay, 1993.

Letters and Sounds Assessment

C	Z	W	S	X	E	D
A	R	F	V	T	G	B
Y	H	N	U	J	M	I
K	O	L	P	Q		
a	c	z	w	s	x	e
d	a	r	f	v	t	g
b	y	h	n	u	j	m
i	k	o	l	p	q	g

wh	th	ch	sh

Analyzing the Results: Letters and Sounds

When the assessment is finished add the total number of letters named correctly, number of correct letter sounds, and the number of correct words for each letter. Determining whether responses to the vowel sounds are correct or incorrect can be a bit tricky. It may or may not be acceptable if the child says the short sound for the vowel but gives a word that begins with the long vowel sound. For example, the child says /ā/ and gives the word apple. It may be necessary to ask the child if the two have the same sound. "Do /ā/ and apple begin with the same sound?" If you are still unsure ask the child for other words that begin with the sound for a.

Next complete the far right column. List the letters that the child was unable to identify by name. Then list the letter sounds that the child was unable to identify. Be sure to put the sounds between / / to indicate they are sounds.

Record student responses in each of the letters and sounds column of the Phonemic Awareness/Letters and Sounds Summary. Put the number of letters, sounds, and words the child was able to identify.

Once all of the students' responses have been recorded, look at the number of correct responses. It will be necessary to determine what an appropriate number of correct responses might be. For example, if you are working with second grade children you will expect them to know all of their letter names. If they can correctly identify all of the consonant sounds but are unable to correctly identify all of the vowel sounds, that may or may not be acceptable. However, if you are working with early first graders it may be acceptable that they know 20 letter names and you will want to work with children that know fewer than 20. You would not expect early first graders to know all of their letter sounds, particularly the vowel sounds. It is important to note that many young children have difficulty hearing and segmenting vowel sounds. It is not necessary to know vowel sounds to be able to successfully read and understand text. For example, you can read and understand this sentence:

Y cn d yr hmwrk ltr.

Older children should be exposed to vowels and sounds but not held back from reading if they do not successfully know all of them.

After an acceptable level has been determined use a highlighting marker to indicate the children that are unable to meet those criteria. Once all of the skills are highlighted, look at the students that need assistance. Students with similar needs should come together as a group to work on learning about that print concept. These groups should be flexible. Once a student is able to demonstrate the skill she should no longer be a member of the group.

There are suggested activities in Chapter Three for practicing letters and sounds.

Assessing Readers

- Does he have a vocabulary of words that he knows by sight?

  Administer the Ohio Word Test or the graded sentences section of an informal reading inventory.

- Can he read grade-level material? Does he comprehend grade-level materials?

  Administer a running record or an informal reading inventory.

- Does he have good decoding skills?

  Look at the errors made on the running record or an informal reading inventory.

- Does he attend to the meaning of what he is reading?

  Look at the errors made on the running record or an informal reading inventory.

  Ask comprehension questions after each selection.

- Does he guess at word meaning?

  Ask about specific vocabulary in each selection.

- Does he read fluently?

  Listen to the child read aloud and note fluency.

- Does he use what he knows about the English language (grammar, syntax) to help him understand what he is reading?

  Look at the cues used on the running record or an informal reading inventory.

Administering the Assessment: Ohio Word Test

Good readers automatically read many words by sight. This allows the reader to focus on the meaning of the text rather than having to decode each individual word.

Knowing how many words a reader has in her sight vocabulary can help us better understand how to help her become a better reader. The Ohio Word Test (Pinnell, Lyons, Young, and Deford, 1987) asks children to read high-frequency words to determine his or her sight vocabulary.

Make a copy of page 28. You may also want to use a "window" like the one used on the letters and sounds assessment. To make a "window" cut a piece of tag board to 11" x 4". Then cut a small square (1" x $\frac{1}{2}$") out of the rectangle about $\frac{1}{4}$ of the way from the top. This will allow the child to see only one word at a time as they read from the list.

You will need a copy of page 27 to record what the child reads.

1. Show the child the lists of words on page 28.
2. Allow the child to choose a list of words to read OR ask the child to read one of the lists of words.
3. Place a ✓ by each word the child reads correctly.
4. If the child reads the word incorrectly write what she says.
5. If the child does not respond put a (beside the word. If she looks at you for assistance ask her if she knows the word. If she says "no" place a (beside the word and ask her to continue reading.

Ohio Word Test

Date________________

Student Name______________________ Recorder______________________ Grade__________

Choose one list of words for the student to read.

Correct Response ✓ Record Incorrect Responses No Response •

List A	List B	List C
and	ran	big
the	it	to
pretty	said	ride
has	her	him
down	find	for
where	we	you
after	they	this
let	live	may
here	away	in
am	are	at
there	no	with
over	put	some
little	look	make
did	do	eat
what	who	an
them	then	walk
one	play	red
like	again	now
could	give	from
yes	saw	have
Number Correct /20	/20	/20

used with permission from Gay Su Pinnell

Ohio Word Test

List A	List B	List C
and	ran	big
the	it	to
pretty	said	ride
has	her	him
down	find	for
where	we	you
after	they	this
let	live	may
here	away	in
am	are	at
there	no	with
over	put	some
little	look	make
did	do	eat
what	who	an
them	then	walk
one	play	red
like	again	now
could	give	from
yes	saw	have

Running Record/Informal Reading Inventory Summary

Teacher	Date

Student Name	Ohio Word Test	Word Recognition (RR & IRI)			Info. Used (MSV)	Comprehension (IRI)			Fluency
		Indep. Level	Instr. Level	Frust. Level		Indep. Level	Instr. Level	Frust. Level	

Analyzing the Results: Ohio Word Test

Identify the number of words the child read correctly at the bottom of the page. Record that information on the Running Record/Informal Reading Inventory Summary. Once all of the students' responses have been recorded look at the number of correct responses. It will be necessary to determine what an appropriate number of correct responses might be. For example, if you are working with second-grade children you will expect them to know all of the sight words on a list. However, if you are working with early first graders it may be acceptable that they know 10 of the sight words, and you will want to work with children that know fewer than 10.

You will also want to look at the words that they read incorrectly. If he read 10 words correctly and made ten errors, the errors will tell you what he knows about reading new words. If all of his words (the ones that were incorrect) began with the same sound as the word on the list, then you can assume he knows about beginning sounds. For example, if he said *please* for *pretty*, *dog* for *down*, *water* for *where*, and *time* for *there* then you know he understands beginning sounds and is ready for more information on blends and digraphs. If he said *party* for *pretty*, *dawn* for *down*, *what* for *where*, and *this* for *there* you can assume he knows about consonant sounds and may be ready for information about vowel sounds.

You will need to look carefully at what each child understands about reading words before you can place them in a group. The information from this assessment may (should) confirm groups that are already formed based on information from previous assessments.

If the child is unable to read any of the words he should probably be in a group working with other children on letters and sounds and learning words on the word wall. If the child reads a few of the words and his errors show that he knows about beginning sounds, he should probably be in a group with other children reading and working with words on the word wall. The best way to reinforce learning to read words is to read with children every day. Each group, regardless of what they are practicing, should spend some time reading every day.

There are specific activities for reading with children in Chapter Two and learning words in Chapter Five.

Administering the Assessment: Running Records and Informal Reading Inventories

Informal reading inventories and running records are written records of the student's oral reading as observed and recorded by the instructor. Students read orally as the instructor records the student's correct and incorrect responses.

Informal reading inventories are given occasionally, generally at the beginning and end of the year. The informal reading inventory is designed to determine a child's reading level, specific strengths and weaknesses in word recognition, and reading comprehension. This is determined by analyzing the student's correct and incorrect responses that are recorded by the instructor as the student reads orally. The informal reading inventory is a purchased set of graded stories and questions. There are many informal reading inventories available for purchase. Some suggested criteria and informal reading inventories are listed on pages 8 and 9.

Running records (Clay, 1993) should be taken on a regular basis as part of the ongoing assessment process. A running record can be taken with any reading material. With practice, the instructor can take a running record any place at any time. An analysis of the running record can inform instruction by:

- evaluating text difficulty
- informing how children can be grouped
- accelerating a child's instruction
- monitoring the progress of children
- allowing different children to move through different texts at different speeds
- observing specific difficulties in children

Begin informal reading inventories at a point where you believe the child will be successful. If you think the child reads at the third-grade level, then ask him to read the first- or second-grade sentences and selection in the informal reading inventory or a book at the first or second grade level. If you think the child is a reader at the first-grade level, the informal reading inventory may be a bit challenging to start with so ask him to tell you the sounds of the letters of the alphabet before you ask him to read a list of sight words or words in context.

Running records may be taken on new or familiar reading material. If a child reads a book that is new to him, it should be at a level you believe he will be successful. It is better to err on the side of "easy" rather than hard. A running record of new material will give you information about his independent and/or instructional reading level and how well he reads, decodes, and understands new material. If you ask him to read a book he has practiced, it should give you information about the appropriateness of the level of the material and how well he has developed fluency.

Blank copies of a Running Record form may be found on page 33. This form may be used to transcribe a piece of text so that you might follow along as the student reads. Because it is time-consuming to transcribe each piece of text and it requires knowing in advance what text the child will be reading, it may be more helpful to use a blank form to record student responses. To do this requires that you sit next to the child and follow along in her text as you record the error and the correct word.

The recording and analysis of the running record and the informal reading inventory are the same. The instructor records what students say as they are reading. Do not worry about what they are saying–simply get it down. You will analyze their responses after the session. The following information shows how to record what student say as they are reading.

How to Mark the Informal Reading Inventory and Running Record

1. Mark every word read correctly with a check mark.

✓	✓	✓	✓	✓	✓	✓	✓	✓	✓	✓	✓	
Huge	balloons	sailed	over	the	hill	and	drifted	toward	the	open	field.	no error

2. Record a wrong response by writing the word read by the child over the text.

High	✓	✓	✓	✓	✓	✓	✓	✓	✓	✓	✓	
Huge	balloons	sailed	over	the	hill	and	drifted	toward	the	open	field.	one error

3. If a child tries several times to read a word, record all of his trials.

								town				
✓	✓	✓	✓	✓	✓	✓	✓	to	✓	✓	✓	
Huge	balloons	sailed	over	the	hill	and	drifted	toward	the	open	field.	one error

4. If a child is able to correct an error this is recorded as a "self-correction," and NOT an error.

								town SC				
✓	✓	✓	✓	✓	✓	✓	✓	to	✓	✓	✓	
Huge	balloons	sailed	over	the	hill	and	drifted	toward	the	open	field.	no error

5. If a word is omitted it is marked with a dash.

✓	✓	✓	✓	✓	✓	✓	✓	✓	✓	–	✓	
Huge	balloons	sailed	over	the	hill	and	drifted	toward	the	open	field.	one error

If a word is added it is recorded over a dash.

							slowly						
✓	✓	✓	✓	✓	✓	✓	–	✓	✓	✓	✓	✓	
Huge	balloons	sailed	over	the	hill	and		drifted	toward	the	open	field.	one error

6. If the child stops and is unable to continue because he is aware he has made an error and cannot correct it, or because he does not know how to read the next word, he is told the word. It is marked with a T.

✓	✓	T	✓	✓	✓	✓	✓	✓	✓	✓	✓	
Huge	balloons	sailed	over	the	hill	and	drifted	toward	the	open	field.	one error

7. A child may seek help by asking for help or simply looking at the instructor for assistance. An appeal for help is first given back to the child for further effort. If he is still unable to proceed, tell him the word and mark it A (appeal) and T (told).

✓	✓	A/T	✓	✓	✓	✓	✓	✓	✓	✓	✓	
Huge	balloons	sailed	over	the	hill	and	drifted	toward	the	open	field.	one error

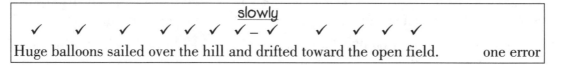

8. If the child gets completely confused you can say, "Try that again." Mark the text to be read again with large brackets and then mark the passage TTA (try that again). Analyze the second attempt, not the first.

✓	✓	A/T	✓	✓	✓	✓	✓	✓	✓	✓	✓	
Hug	balls	A/T	✓	✓	✓	✓	drew	to	✓	–	A/T	TTA
Huge	balloons	sailed	over	the	hill	and	drifted	toward	the	open	field.	one error

9. Repetition is not counted as an error, but it is recorded. Repetition is recorded with an arrow showing the portion of the text that was reread. Analyze the second reading, not the first.

✓	✓	A/T	✓	✓	✓	✓	✓	✓	✓	✓	✓	
Hug	balls	A/T										
Huge	balloons	sailed	over	the	hill	and	drifted	toward	the	open	field.	one error

10. A word that is repeated in the passage is counted wrong every time it is read incorrectly. The only time this is not true is if the word is a proper noun. Proper nouns are counted wrong the first time only.

✓	✓	✓	✓	to	✓	✓	✓	✓	to	✓	✓	
Huge	balloons	sailed	over	the	hill	and	drifted	toward	the	open	field.	two errors

11. Words that are pronounced differently by the child because of dialect are not counted as errors.

✓	✓	✓	✓	✓	✓	✓	✓	tord	✓	✓	✓	
Huge	balloons	sailed	over	the	hill	and	drifted	toward	the	open	field.	no errors

End the session by saying "Tell me about the story." Record what the child says. This will emphasize the need for comprehension and give you an informal assessment as to how well the student understood what was read.

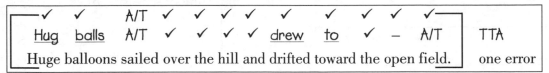

Running Record

Name ______________________________

Text Title ____________________________

Recorder ____________________________

Date _________________________________

Number of Words Read: __________

Percent Correct:

95%-100%	Independent
90%-95%	Instructional
>89%	Frustration

Text	# of E	# of SC	Information Used E MSV	Information Used SC MSV

Tell me about the story.

Running Record

Name Judy

Text Title My Dog Joe

Recorder Karen

Date October 4, 2002

Number of Words Read: 106

Percent Correct:

95%-100%	Independent
90%-95%	Instructional
>89% (circled)	Frustration (circled)

Text	# of E	# of SC	Information Used	
			E MSV	SC MSV
✓ ✓ ✓ ✓ ✓ ✓ ✓ My dog Joe is big and red.				
✓ ✓ ✓ ✓ ✓ I'm glad he's my dog.				
✓ ✓ can ✓ ✓ ✓ ✓ ✓ joe higher My dog knows how to run fast and jump high.	3		V	
✓ ✓ ✓ ✓ ✓ ✓ my ✓ My dog eats dog food and people food.	1		M	
✓ ✓ ✓ ✓ ✓ ✓ – ✓ ✓ the[SC] yard My dog knows how to dig big holes in Mom's garden.	2	1	M	V
✓ ✓ ✓ ✓ ✓ ✓ in ✓ ✓ ✓ ✓ My dog knows how to find interesting things in the yard.	1		V	
✓ ✓ ✓ ✓ ✓ the ✓ A/T My dog is afraid of thunder and lightning.	2		V	
✓ ✓ ✓ ✓ ✓ it is ✓ ✓ ✓ ✓ But I'm not. I know it's only the weather outside	1		MS	
✓ ✓ won't ✓ ✓ ✓ ✓ ✓ and it can't come in and get me.	1		MS	
✓ ✓ ✓ ✓ ✓ ✓ ✓ liked[SC] ✓ ✓ I gave Joe a big hug. He licked my face.		1	V	M
✓ ✓ ✓ ✓ ✓ ✓ ✓ ✓ ✓ ✓ "I'm glad you're my dog," I told my dog Joe.				
✓ ✓ ✓ ✓ ✓ ✓ ✓ ✓ I think he's glad he's my dog, too.				

Tell me about the story. 11

Analyzing the Results: Running Records and Informal Reading Inventories

Running Records

Once the session is complete count the number of errors and the number of self-corrections that were made. Record that information in the two columns at the end of the line of text. To determine the accuracy of the reading, count the errors and subtract that number from the total number of words in the passage. This will give you the total number of words read correctly. Divide the number of words read correctly by the number of words in the passage. This will tell whether the passage is at his independent reading level (95% accuracy), instructional reading level (90% accuracy), or frustration level (less than 90% accuracy).

Record the level of the passage at his independent reading level, instructional reading level, or frustration level under the word recognition (RR & IRI) column on the Running Record/Informal Reading Inventory Summary.

Informal Reading Inventories

A purchased reading inventory will have many of these formulas calculated. Determine the reading level then look at the errors the child made.

Record the level of the passage at his independent reading level, instructional reading level, or frustration level under the word recognition (RR & IRI) column and comprehension column on the Running Record/Informal Reading Inventory Summary.

Running Records and Informal Reading Inventories

Proficient readers use three sources of information when they come to a word they don't know: meaning, structure, and visual (Clay, 1993). They use all three sources or cues simultaneously. When a proficient reader comes to a word she doesn't know she looks at the beginning sound(s) of the new word and thinks about what makes sense and fits grammatically. This is done very quickly, and the reader is usually unaware that she is doing it. Struggling readers typically rely on one information source over the others.

Look at the errors the child made on the running record or the informal reading inventory. At the end of each line of text determine which information source students *used*. This helps you determine what students are paying attention to and what strategies they are using. This will guide the intervention you will use. It is important to remember that we are looking at what information was used, not the information that was not used.

- Meaning

  Does the word(s) the child substituted make sense? If what he reads makes sense, even though it is inaccurate, then he is probably more focused on meaning than visual (letters and sounds) or structural (grammar) cues. Meaning cues may come from pictures, previous text, and/or the general meaning of the story.

✓	✓	came	✓	✓	✓	✓	✓	✓	✓	✓	✓
Huge	balloons	sailed	over	the	hill	and	drifted	toward	the	open	field.

  This is an example of an error that might be labeled meaning. The word *came* is incorrect, but it does not change the meaning of the sentence. The child is using meaning to read an unfamiliar word.

- Structure/Grammar

  Is what he said grammatically correct (up to and including the substitution)? If it is, his speaking vocabulary may be influencing his response.

✓	✓	✓	✓	✓	✓	✓	✓	<u>high</u>	✓	✓	✓
Huge	balloons	sailed	over	the	hill	and	drifted	toward	the	open	field.

  This is an example of an error that might be labeled structural. The word *high* is grammatically correct up to the error, so the student is using his knowledge of grammar to read the sentence. However, he is not attending to the visual cues in the word *toward* or to the meaning of the remaining words in the sentence.

- Visual/Letter Sound Association

  Does he use information about the way the letters and words look? If the word he says looks similar to the word in the passage, he is using visual cues to help him read words that are unfamiliar to him. For example, if the word he says begins with the same sound as the word in the passage, he is using letter sounds as the visual cue.

<u>High</u>	✓	✓	✓	✓	✓	✓	✓	✓	✓	✓	✓
Huge	balloons	sailed	over	the	hill	and	drifted	toward	the	open	field.

  This is an example of an error that might be labeled visual. The word *high* looks like *huge* and begins with the same sound. The child is using what he knows about letters, sounds, and words to read an unfamiliar word.

Most often a child that reads for meaning is also attending to the structure or grammar of the sentence. It may be difficult to separate the two. If so, it may be appropriate to mark both. See the sample Running Record on page 34 for marking examples.

Now look at the self-corrections the child made. At the end of each line of text, determine which information source was used that made the error. Record this under E MSV. Then, look at which information source was used to make the self-correction. Record this under SC MSV. This will tell you which information source they use to correct their errors. For example, in the sample Running Record on page 35 the child said *liked* for *licked*. This would be a visual error since they are visually similar. When she self-corrected she used meaning to determine that *liked my face* didn't make sense, so she corrected it so say *licked*.

It is important to note that analyzing student responses is not an easy task. There will be many ways to label an error and many differences of opinion about what is correct. It is most important to look at the pattern of errors. Does the student seem to rely primarily on one source of information over the others? A good reader will use all three sources while reading unfamiliar words and passages. Relying too heavily on one system over the others will create a reader who simply calls words or one who substitutes words without attending to any visual information. Knowing what cueing system a child relies on will help you determine how to intervene to develop the other systems not in use.

If a student is relying primarily on meaning, it will be beneficial to support his reading with strategies that promote looking at letters and sounds. "You said, 'came.' Does *came* begin with that sound (a)?"

If a reader is relying primarily on structure, it will be beneficial to support her reading with strategies that promote meaning and visual cues. "You said, 'high.' Does *high* begin with that sound? Does it make sense with the rest of the sentence?"

If a child is relying primarily on visual cues, it will be beneficial to support his reading with strategies that promote meaning and structure. "You said, 'high.' Does *high* make sense? Would we say it that way?"

Chapter Two has suggestions for activities that will promote reading for meaning and structure. Chapter Three has suggestions that will promote attending to visual cues. All three cueing systems are reinforced in the Guess the Covered Word activity in Chapter Four.

Additional Assessment Information

Word Meaning

If children do not pay attention to the meaning of the words they are reading, they are simply calling the words on the page. To determine how well the student uses word meaning as a strategy ask him to tell you about specific vocabulary in each selection. For example, if students are reading information on habitats they may encounter words such as: *hydrosphere*, *atmosphere*, *biodiversity*, *non-renewable resources*, *transpiration*, or *lithosphere*.

There are suggested activities that develop vocabulary in Chapter Five.

Fluency

Fluency is how quickly, accurately, and expressively students read a text. A fluent reader reads as though she is telling the story. A student's fluency affects her comprehension, attitude toward reading, and willingness to read for pleasure. A child that reads slowly, sounding out each new word she sees with many hesitations, loses the meaning of what she is reading. She also sees reading as a difficult task and tries to avoid it if possible. Children typically develop fluency in reading in the second or third grade.

To informally determine the child's literacy rate, listen to the child read a passage aloud. This may be done as a part of a running record or informal reading inventory. Make a notation about the child's fluency:

- Does she read smoothly, in large meaningful phrases with accurate expression? Note that her reading is fluent.
- Is her reading smooth and somewhat expressive with hesitations for meaning and vocabulary? Note that she is developing fluency.
- Is her reading mostly word-by-word with multiple hesitations and little expression? Note that her reading is word-by-word with little fluency.

Suggestions for developing fluency can be found in Chapter Two.

Planning for Instruction

Results of the reading profile will assist instructors in creating small, flexible groups of children. The small groups are designed to deliver intense instruction in one or two skills or strategies to accelerate the reader's development. This is a support to the regular classroom instruction and not a replacement. The groups students work with should be small and flexible. Groups should not be any larger than three to five children. When students are capable of more complex reading and writing, groups should be reconfigured. Some children will no longer need small group support. Some children will need less support. Other children will need continued support, but the emphasis will be on new skills and strategies.

Groups should meet daily if possible. If a 30-minute time block is available time should be divided by:

- 10 minutes working with Guided Reading strategies,
- 10 minutes with Working with Sound and Letter Relationship Strategies OR Learning Words Strategies and Decoding New Words, and
- 10 minutes Writing.

Be sure you are reading daily! If you only have 20 minutes to spend with students, then alternate Working with Sound and Letter Relationship Strategies or Learning Words Strategies and Decoding New Words with Writing. A group should never meet without actually reading a book.

The books you choose to read with the group should match their instructional reading level (found by administering an informal reading inventory). A good resource for selecting books at any given level is *Matching Books to Readers : Using Leveled Books in Guided Reading, K-3* (Fountas and Pinnell, 1999). This resource is filled with titles at levels A-P for readers in grades K-3. To assist in selecting books, the following grade-level equivalents have been established:

Level	Approximate Grade Level	Level	Approximate Grade Level
A	Kindergarten/Grade One	**K**	Grade Two (early)
B	Kindergarten/Grade One	**L**	Grade Two
C	Grade One	**M**	Grade Two
D	Grade One	**N**	Grade Two
E	Grade One	**O**	Grade Three
F	Grade One	**P**	Grade Three
G	Grade One	**Q**	Grade Three
H	Grade One	**R**	Grade Four (early)
I	Grade One	**S**	Grade Four (late)
J	Grade One (late)		

The plan for each group should look different. The skills and strategies to be taught will be determined by the results of the reading profile. The time you spend with students is valuable. What you do in the group must be well designed and targeted to meet each student's needs. Be sure to have the materials you need prepared and readily available.

The makeup of each group should change often as the children in the group show that they are capable of using the targeted skill or strategy on their own. Flexible groups allow you to deliver quality support only as long as children need that support. It also allows you to move the learner on to the next thing he needs to know to be a fluent reader.

Groups should meet regularly. The amount of support needed by the children in the group will determine how often the group meets. Groups of children that are reading significantly below grade level should meet more often and for longer periods of time than groups that need only some support.

Reading

Chapter Two

Working with children in small flexible groups on the skills they need to become better readers is an important part of the teaching process. Plans should be carefully designed so that each child spends time doing what is most beneficial to them. Sometimes it is easy to forget that the purpose of the group meeting is to be a better reader, not a better "skiller." Children should read or be read to every time the group meets. Actual reading takes a priority over all other activities. Students should not spend time doing activities about reading without really reading.

Reading to, with, and by Children

Students with little reading experience or those with reading difficulties need many opportunities to be read to, be read with, and read by themselves. Children should spend some time each day engaged in each activity. The amount of time you spend reading to or with children or the amount of time they read by themselves may be determined by the child's reading skills and reading level.

You will spend more time reading to children with few print concepts and little knowledge of the alphabet. You will spend some time reading to children with print concepts and letter identification and few letter/sound relationships. You will spend less time reading to children with print concepts, letter/sound relationships, and a small sight vocabulary.

All children will benefit from you reading with them. This may be accomplished by having students echo what you read or by choral reading together. More time will be spent reading with children with reading difficulties than those without.

Children should read on their own for a portion of each day, including children with few print concepts. Looking at books and "pretend" reading reinforces the skills and strategies you will be introducing to them. Due to the limited time you will have to spend with children in a small, flexible group, it may be best that you spend that time reading to and with children. If you are pushing in you can reinforce children reading by themselves in the classroom while the whole class is engaged by being available to assist and/or answer questions.

Learning about Print Concepts

Reading to and with Children

As you read to and with children you can reinforce the concepts about print that children need to understand. This particular activity should recreate a comfortable reading with a child sitting on your lap. One of the important parts of this reading is looking at the book together. This may be best modeled with several children by using a big book. If you are working with only a few children you may use a "small" book. You will want them to sit around you so they can easily see the text.

- Discuss the cover of the book including the title, author, and illustrator. Have children discuss the illustrations and make predictions about the story.

- Turn to the title page and discuss the information it contains. There is information about the title and author as well as the publisher. Reinforce that this is not the first page of the story.

- Show children the first page of the story. Discuss how you know it is the first page of the story and not the cover or the title page (print, pictures, etc.). Tell children this is where you will begin reading the story to them.

- Before you begin reading, tell them you will be reading from the left to the right. You will point to each word as you read it to them. This will help you keep track of where you are.

- Ask children what they should do while you read. Ideally, they will respond with listening, paying attention, and enjoying the story.

- At the end of the first page, show children that you will turn one page and will begin reading on the left facing page so you don't miss any of the story.

- Continue reading the story, pointing to the words as you read.

- At the end of the reading, ask children to tell you about the story. After hearing what students have to say, tell them what you think the story is about. Be sure this is not the "right" answer, but is simply your thoughts.

By doing these activities every time you read to or with children they will become more familiar with print concepts. Eventually, you will only need to refer to these occasionally and will spend more time on other concepts they need to learn.

Developing Reading Comprehension

Reading with Children - Story Book or Poem (Levels A-M; PP-Grade 2)

Choose a book or poem at the students' instructional reading level. *Matching Books to Readers: Using Leveled Books in Guided Reading, K-3* (Fountas and Pinnell, 1999) is an excellent resource for identifying books at a variety of reading levels. There are also many sites on the Internet that list books by levels (a list of Web sites is on page 102).

If it takes longer than 7-10 minutes to read, plan to read a portion of it each day so that time remains to discuss what was read.

Here is a suggested guide for each time you read the story. The different activities have children do something before they read the story, while they read the story, and after they read the story. Notice that each story should be read several times. This allows children to focus on different aspects of the story and will aid in the development of fluency.

First Reading:

1. Picture Walk
2. Read Aloud -OR- Echo Read
3. Discuss Story

Second Reading:

1. Echo Read -OR- Choral Read
2. Discuss Story -OR- Retell Story -OR- Draw after Reading

Third Reading:

1. Choral Read -OR- Partner Read -OR- Character Read
2. Discuss Story -OR- Work with Story

Fourth Reading:

1. Partner Read -OR- Character Read -OR- Read Favorite Part/Favorite Page
2. Work with Story

First Reading

Purpose: To introduce the story to students and have them begin thinking about what is going to happen in the story.

1. Picture Walk

Purpose:

- To get students to begin thinking about the story. This allows students to use whatever knowledge they have about the topic to "guess" what will happen. This prediction sets the purpose for reading the book–to see if they are correct.
- To teach important vocabulary or concepts that will help students understand the story.

Look at the picture on each page. Ask students to guess what is happening. Ask questions to promote their thinking about the pictures (you may write down their predictions if it helps you keep track). Identify anything that might be an obstacle to students' understanding of the story.

Note: If students predict incorrectly, that is okay. Don't try to correct them or ask them leading questions to get them to the "right" answer.

2. Read Aloud

Purpose: To model correct reading and fluency and promote comprehension. (You may want to read the story to children for the first reading if it appears to be slightly difficult for them.)

The instructor reads the story to children as children follow along. Take time to think aloud about things happening in the story as you read. If students are following along with their own text they should be tracking the print by pointing to each word as it is read.

-OR-

Echo Read

Purpose: To model correct reading and fluency and promote comprehension. (You may choose to have children echo the story after you for the first reading if it is slightly easier to understand with fewer words and less difficult vocabulary.)

The instructor reads a sentence fluently with expression. Students echo the sentence mimicking the instructor's reading pattern. If students are following along with their own text, they should be tracking the print by pointing to each word as it is read.

3. Discuss Story

Purpose: Check predictions to promote comprehension.

Begin by asking, "What did you think?" Allow students to share whatever thoughts come to mind.

Then have students discuss their original predictions and compare them to what actually happened in the story. Focus on what picture clues provided accurate information and what caused students to make incorrect predictions. Don't focus on which student was correct or incorrect.

Note: If there is not enough time to do the Picture Walk, Echo Read, and Discussion, do the Picture Walk first and record their predictions. Agree that you will read the text together tomorrow to find out if they are correct or not.

Second Reading:

Purpose: Review the predictions and story events and continue to practice fluency and comprehension.

1. **Echo Read**

-OR-

Choral Read

Purpose: To provide voice support to students as they practice reading a text with intonation and fluency.

Everyone (including the instructor) reads the text together. The instructor is "guiding" the reading by reading with fluency and expression.

Note: If students misread words or stumble, don't stop the reading or call attention to them. They are in the practice stage, and you are still modeling for them.

2. **Discuss Story**

Allow students an opportunity to talk about what was read. Be sure to ask questions that do not have one right or wrong answer. Some questions you might want to use are:

- What was an important problem in this story?
- How was the problem solved?
- Has anything like this ever happened to you? Tell us about it.
- What is the author trying to tell us?
- Why do you think the author told this story?
- What would you tell a friend about this story?
- Were any of our predictions correct?

-OR-

Retell Story

Have students pretend you did not read the story with them. Have them retell it to you in their own words.

-OR-

Draw after Reading

Have students draw a picture that illustrates an important event in the story. Allow time for each student to share and tell about their drawing.

Third Reading:

Purpose: Further develop fluency and comprehension.

1. **Choral Read**

-OR-

Partner Read

Purpose: To allow students to share a story with another reader so they can share their ideas and help one another.

Students read the story with a partner. One partner reads one page and then the other partner reads the next.

-OR-

Character Read

Purpose: To assist comprehension.

Students read the story as if the characters were speaking. The instructor needs to "direct" the experience. The instructor (or a student) takes the part of the narrator. If there are more parts (characters) than students, the instructor can read some of them. If there are fewer parts than students, they can partner with others and choral read the part together.

2. **Discuss Story**

Choose questions not discussed previously.

-OR-

Have students bring interesting questions to the group. At first you may find that they ask rather simple, factual questions. As time passes and you continue modeling good questions, students' questions will become more complex and interesting.

-OR-

Work with Story

Purpose: Further develop students' comprehension of the story.

Story Sequence:

- Students create a three- or four-frame cartoon that retells the story. This can be done individually or with each student taking a part to sequence (beginning, middle, end).
- Three or four students stand. Each tells the part that corresponds to their place in the line.
- Students write or draw the sequence of events and then link the writing/drawing by lines or links.

Main Idea

- The instructor thinks out loud as she models how to find the one "big" thing the story is about.
- Students think along with the instructor as she asks questions to find out the one "big" thing the story is about.
- Brainstorm other titles for the story.

Compare/Contrast

- Students create a Venn Diagram to compare/contrast (same/different) parts of the story. They may compare/contrast characters, settings, or events within one story or they may compare/contrast two stories.

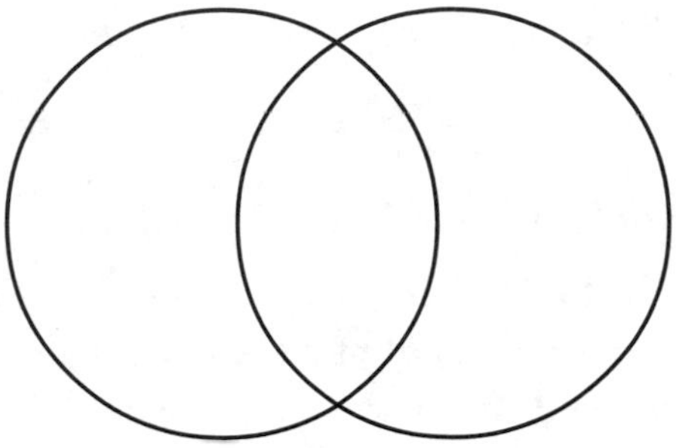

- Identify two character or events from a story. Have students fold a piece of paper into four parts. In the first two boxes have them show how the two characters/events are the same and in the last two boxes how they are different.

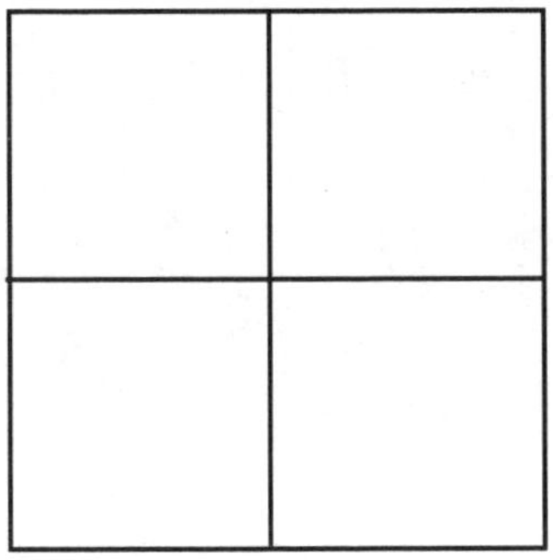

Fourth Reading:

Purpose: To complete the book and bring some closure to the experience.

1. **Partner Read**

-OR-

Character Read

-OR-

Have students read their favorite part or favorite page. Ask them to tell why it is their favorite.

2. **Work with Story**

   Select one activity that students have not already completed and that would help them better understand the story.

Reading with Children - Chapter Book (Levels K-P; Gr.2-Gr.3)

Choose a chapter book, story, or poem at the students' instructional reading level. The reading activities for a chapter book are planned chapter by chapter. It should take approximately two days to read each chapter. This includes the rereading practice students need. If it takes longer than 7-10 minutes to read the chapter, plan to read a portion of it each day so that time remains to discuss the book. The different activities have children do something before they read the story, while they read the story, and after they read the story.

Introducing the Book

1. **Picture Walk** -OR- **Table of Contents Hunt**
2. **Read Aloud** -OR- **Echo Read**
3. **Discuss Story**

Reading Each Chapter

First Reading:

1. **Read Aloud**
2. **Choral Read**
3. **Discuss Story**

Second Reading:

1. **Partner Read** -OR- **Character Read**
2. **Discuss Story** -OR- **Work with Story**

Introducing the Book

Purpose: To introduce the story to students and begin thinking about what is going to happen in the story.

1. Picture Walk

Purpose:

- To get students to begin thinking about the story. This allows students to use whatever knowledge they have about the topic to "guess" what will happen. This prediction sets the purpose for reading the book–to see if they are correct.
- To teach important vocabulary or concepts that will help students understand the story.

Look at the picture on the cover. Ask students to guess what is happening. Flip through the book and see if there are any other pictures. Ask questions to promote their thinking about the pictures (you may write down their predictions if it helps you keep track). Identify anything that might be an obstacle to students understanding the story.

Note: If students predict incorrectly, that is okay. Don't try to correct them or ask them leading questions to get them to the "right" answer.

-OR-

Table of Contents Hunt

Purpose: Make predictions about the story.

Have students find the table of contents. Allow them to make predictions about the story based on chapter titles. Be sure to ask them why.

Note: If students predict incorrectly, that is okay. Don't try to correct them or ask them leading questions to get them to the "right" answer.

Reading Each Chapter

First Reading:

1. Read Aloud

Purpose: To model correct reading and fluency and promote comprehension.

The instructor reads the first few pages of the chapter to children as the children follow along. Take time to think aloud about things happening in the story as you read. If students are following along with their own text they should be tracking the print by pointing to each word as it is read.

2. Choral Read

Purpose: To provide voice support to students as they practice reading a text with intonation and fluency.

Everyone (including the instructor) reads the rest of the chapter together. The instructor is "guiding" the reading by reading with fluency and expression.

Note: If students misread words or stumble, don't stop the reading or call attention to them. They are in the practice stage, and you are still modeling for them.

3. **Discuss Story**

Some questions you might want to use are:

- What was an important problem in this story?
- How was the problem solved?
- Has anything like this ever happened to you? Tell us about it.
- What is the author trying to tell us?
- Why do you think the author told this story?
- What would you tell a friend about this story?
- Were any of our predictions correct?
- What do you think might happen next?
- Have you changed any of your predictions?

Second Reading:

1. **Partner Read**

Purpose: To allow students to read a story with another student so they can share their ideas and help one another.

Students reread the chapter with a partner. One partner reads one page and then the other partner reads the next.

If time does not allow for students to reread the whole chapter, select four–six pages for them to read with their partner. Ideally, these would be pages that are important to the story and will help them better understand the next chapter.

-OR-

Character Read

Purpose: To assist comprehension.

Students read the story as if the characters were speaking. The instructor needs to "direct" the experience. The instructor (or a student) takes the part of the narrator. If there are more parts (characters) than students, the instructor can read some of them. If there are fewer parts than students, they can partner with others and choral read the part together.

2. Discuss Story

Choose questions not discussed previously.

-OR-

Work with the Story

Purpose: Further develop students' comprehension of the story.

Story Sequence:

- Students create a three- to four-frame cartoon that retells the story. This can be done individually or with each student taking a part to sequence (beginning, middle, end).
- Three or four students stand. Each tells the part that corresponds to their place in the line.
- Students write or draw the sequence of events and then link the writing/drawing by lines or links.

  Note: Identify the completed sequence of events as a summary IF the events chosen were the most important parts.

Main Idea

- The instructor thinks out loud as she models how to find the one "big" thing the story is about.
- Students think along with the instructor as she asks questions to find out the one "big" thing the story is about.
- Brainstorm other titles for the story.

Compare/Contrast

- Students create a Venn Diagram to compare/contrast (same/different) parts of the story. They may compare/contrast characters, settings, or events within one story or they may compare/contrast two stories.
- Identify two character or events from a story. Have students fold a piece of paper into four parts. In the first two boxes have them show how the two characters/events are the same and in the last two boxes how they are different.

Predicting Outcomes

- Have students draw what they think might happen next. Then share the ideas with the group. Refer to the drawings as you continue to read the story.
- Provide students with a summary of the story so far. Then have them write or draw what they think will happen next and how the story will end. This may done as cartoon frames or as a story chain.

Story Elements

- Have students complete a story map identifying the important elements of the story. Complete the map section by section as the story is read.

Title:
Author:
Setting:
Characters:
Problem:
Action: Beginning: Middle: End:
Conclusion:

- Have each member of the small group take responsibility for collecting information about one of the story elements. Provide students with sticky notes to write what they have found. Have them report to the whole group from time to time. Complete a story map at the end with each person's contributions.

Fluency

Fluent readers read quickly, with expression. The reading sounds like "talk" and is easily understood and enjoyed. Patricia Cunningham has several ideas for developing fluency in her book *Phonics They Use* (2000). Some suggestions for developing fluency are:

- Choose books at students' independent reading level. By choosing a book below their instructional level they will spend less time decoding and more time reading fluently with expression. Alternate books that are at students' independent and instructional level to meet the learning needs of all children.
- Use echo reading and choral reading.
- Reread a text several times. Struggling readers may work with the same text for four to seven days.
- Allow older children to practice an easy book to read to a younger child. They may tape the reading of the book to give to a child or a class.
- Have children read into a tape recorder and listen to themselves read. Allow them to critique their own reading before giving it to you to listen. They may choose to reread the same passage over and over again until it sounds right.

Working with Letters & Sounds

Chapter Three

Children should work with sounds and letters daily as they develop phonemic awareness skills. The focus of this time should be on hearing individual sounds in words and learning the names of the letters of the alphabet and their corresponding sound(s).

Developing Phonemic Awareness

Purpose: To identify the order of sounds in spoken words.

Some students need instruction in hearing the sounds within words. A child's phonemic awareness is correlated to his reading success. Phonemic awareness develops in stages, with children progressing through them by paying attention to sounds, not words. Phonemic awareness activities should be done without letters or printed words. The child must hear the word spoken or speak it himself and try to break it into sounds slowly by saying it. If he needs to show what he hears, he should be asked to show what he could hear with counters not letters.

Because we are working with sounds and letters it is important to be able to tell them apart when we are discussing them in print. When the letter stands alone it refers to the name of the letter (v). When the letter comes between two slash marks it refers to the sound of the letter (/v/).

When emphasizing sounds for students it is important that you say the sound clearly and distinctly. For example, when saying the sound for the letter b you should say /b/ not "buh." When you add the "uh" sound at the end you make it difficult for students to later blend sounds into words.

Some identified stages of phonemic awareness (Lundberg, Frost, and Peterson, 1988; Hoffman, Cunningham, and Yopp, 1998; Cooper, 2000) are:

- identifying similarities and differences in a set of spoken words
- identifying and supplying rhyming words
- counting words in sentences
- counting syllables in words
- identifying same beginning sound
- segmenting sounds in words
  - the beginning sound up to the first vowel (onset) and the rest of the word (rime)
  - individual sounds (phonemes)
- blending sounds in words
  - the beginning sound up to the first vowel (onset) and the rest of the word (rime)
  - individual sounds (phonemes)
- substituting sounds to make new words

Although stages may not necessarily develop sequentially some are easier to learn than others. Children will hear the difference in spoken words before they can segment words into individual sounds. After identifying what students know about phonemic awareness, determine which stage students will be most successful learning next.

Suggested Phonemic Awareness Activities

(See pages 55-63 for activity descriptions.)

Stage of Phonemic Awareness		Activity
Identifying similarities and differences in a set of spoken words		Which One Is Different?
		Me!
Counting words in sentences		Counting Words
		How Many words?
Rhyming words	Identify	Matching Game
		Read a Story
	Supply	Read a Story
		Rhyming List
Counting syllables in words		Word Parts
		Choir Practice
Same beginning sound		Which Are the Same?
		Tongue Twisters
Segmenting sounds in words	Initial sound	"Teacher" (song)
		Sounds in Pictures
		Oral Riddles
	Individual sounds	Hearing Sounds in Words
		Popcorn
Blending sounds in words	Initial sound	Beginning and End
		Cheers
	Individual sounds	Putting Sounds Together
		Oral Riddles
Substituting sounds to make new words		Oral Riddles
		How Many Can We Make?

Identifying Similarities and Differences in a Set of Spoken Words

Which One Is Different?

Materials: 3 counters, each of a different color

Say three words in a series. Push a counter as you say each word.

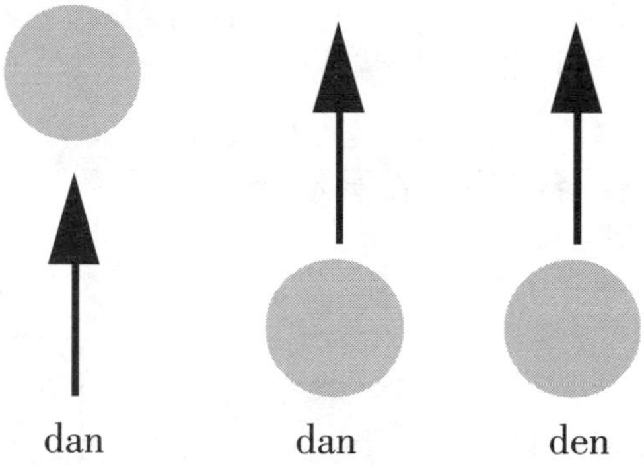

Have students take turns identifying the word that is different by pointing to the correct counter.

Me!

Materials: none

Have three or four children stand up. Point to each child as you say a word. When you are done ask the children not standing, "Who was different?" After hearing from the other children have the child that was "different" announce, "Me!!"

Counting Words in Sentences

Counting Words

Materials: 3-7 counters per child

Give each student a set of counters. Say a short three to four word sentence. Model how to move a counter after you say each word in a sentence.

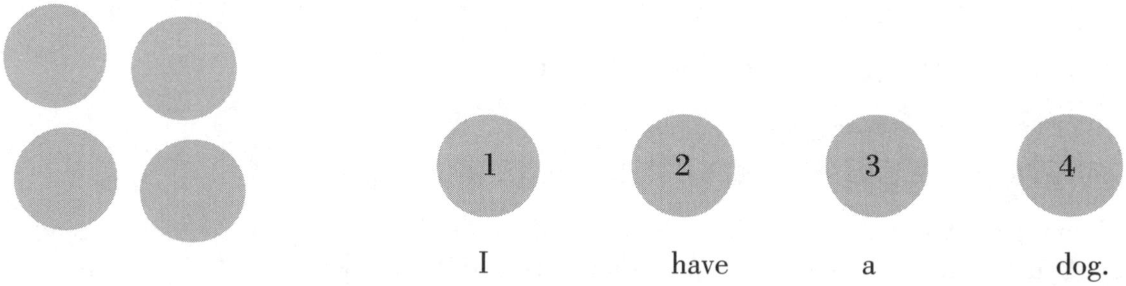

Count how many counters you used, then say another sentence. Have students move counters as you slowly say each word. Then count the number of counters moved.

How Many Words?

Materials: none

Tell students you will be saying a sentence. They are going to stand, one at a time, as you say each word in the sentence. When you are done, ask the next child not standing to count the number of students standing. That is the number of words in your sentence. Begin the next sentence with the next child that did not participate.

Rhyming Words-Identifying Words That Rhyme

Play a Matching Game

Materials: a set of rhyming pictures (page 100)

Place a series of pictures face up. Have students take turns matching two pictures that rhyme. Each student should make one match before the next player takes his turn. If students have difficulty identifying a rhyming pair, then offer to have them choose one picture and you say all of the other picture names, emphasizing the ending sounds so they can find the rhyme.

Read a Rhyming Story or Nursery Rhyme

Materials: a rhyming story or nursery rhyme (a list of rhyming books is on page 127)

Tell students you are going to read a story with rhyming words. As you read be sure to emphasize the rhyming pair. The first time you read the book or nursery rhyme tell them which words rhyme. Then reread the book and have students identify the rhyming words. As students become better at identifying the rhyming words they will be able to identify the rhyming words as you read.

Rhyming Words-Supplying Words That Rhyme

Read a Rhyming Story or Nursery Rhyme

Materials: a rhyming story or nursery rhyme (a list of rhyming books is on page 127)

Select a rhyming story or nursery rhyme to read to students. Tell students you are going to read the story or nursery rhyme up to the rhyming word, and they have to think of a word that finishes the rhyme. Be sure to emphasize the first rhyme in the pair. Have students guess what the rhyming word is. Give the answer by finishing the sentence. Then go back to the beginning of the sentence and reread with all words in place. Encourage students to read along.

A Rhyming List

Materials: a chart, overhead projector, or chalkboard

Tell students you are going to say a word. Have students suggest words that rhyme with the word. After several practice sessions begin to write the rhyming words down. Keep a list of words that rhyme.

book
cook
hook
look
nook*
took
shook

Note: focus on actual words rather than nonsense words

*If the rhyming word is one students may not know use the word in a sentence.

Counting the Number of Syllables in a Word

Word Parts

Materials: none

Tell students that words have parts, and we can count how many parts are in a word by listening as we clap, stomp, or cheer. Start by identifying the syllables in the students' names. Say a name and:

- Clap the syllables.
- Stomp the syllables.
- Cheer the syllables.
- Tap the syllables.

After working with students' names move on to the names of things found in the classroom (desk, window, chair, pencil, crayon, wastebasket, etc.). A list of suggested words for counting syllables is on page 101.

Choir Practice

Materials: none

Once students are able to clap, stomp, or cheer word parts they can direct the syllable choir. Give the "director" a word and a baton. Depending upon the number of syllables in the word, she will tell one or more children to stand. As the director points to them, the children standing will say the corresponding part of the word.

One student:	desk		
Two students:	chil	dren	
Three students:	bas	ket	ball

Identifying Words That Begin with the Same Sound

Which Are the Same?

Materials: three pairs (six cards total) of Beginning Letter Sound Picture Cards (pages 111-115)

Show students one of the picture cards. For example, show the banana card. Then, say the names of the other cards. Stretch out and emphasize the beginning sound of the other cards (e.g., b-e-d; c-a-m-er-a; c-a-ke; d-o-g; d-ough-n-u-t; etc.) Tell students that *banana* and *bed* start alike. Move those two cards off by themselves. Repeat the process with the other cards.

Once you have modeled several times how to listen to the beginning sound, have students listen and then point to the card that starts like the one being matched. Eventually, students should be able to play with more than six cards without you modeling how to stretch out the beginning sound.

Tongue Twisters

Materials: tongue twisters to say to the group (see page 126 for a list of tongue twister books and page 127 for a list of tongue twister Web sites)

Select a short tongue twister that has the same beginning sound as a student in class, such as *Silly Sally sat on Sam*. Have students repeat it after you slowly, then more quickly until it becomes "silly."

Now say it with *Sarah's* name. Have students identify which words in the tongue twister start the same: *silly*, *Sally*, *Sarah*, *sat*, *Sam*. Exaggerate the beginning sounds to help students hear them.

Segmenting the Sounds in a Word-Segmenting the Beginning Sound up to the First Vowel (Onset) and the Rest of the Word (Rime) (e.g., cat is /c/ /at/)

Songs - Teacher (Sung to the Tune of "Bingo")

Materials: none

There was a teacher who had a pet and cat was its name-o.

/c/- /c/- /c/- at

/c/- /c/- /c/- at

/c/- /c/- /c/- at

And cat was its name-o.
(The hard /c/ sound and the /at/ sound are sung, not the names of the letters.)

Other verses:

/d/- /d/- /d/- og

/r/- /r/- /r/- abbit

/h/- /h/- /h/- orse

/g/- /g/- /g/- erbil

/p/- /p/- /p/- ig

Sounds in Pictures

Materials: 2 counters, an index card with two squares drawn on it, several pictures with two- and three-sound words on them (pages 102-104)

Show students a picture card. Model how to say the beginning sound in the picture and move a counter with it. Then, model how to say the rime in the picture and move another counter. Have students repeat after you.

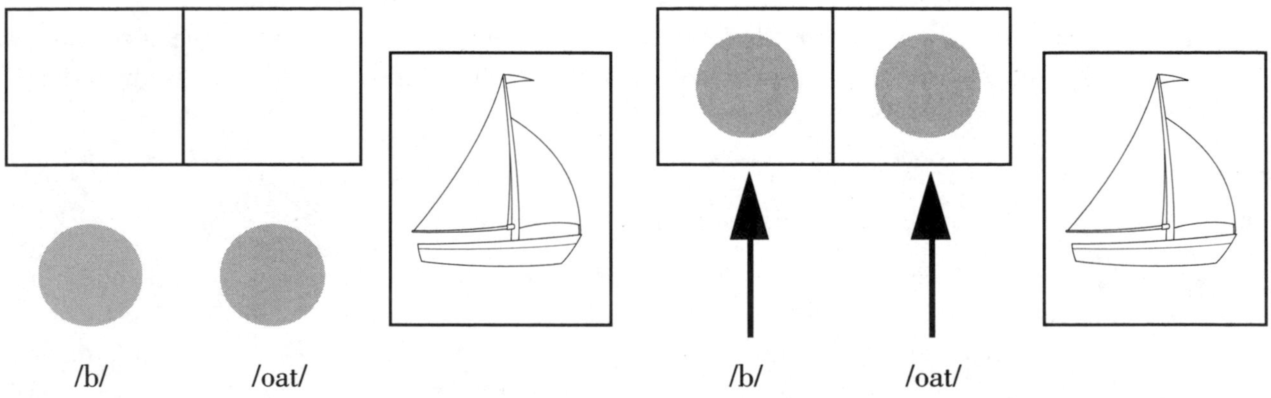

Which Ones Are the Same?

Materials: 2 counters, one green and one red, for every child

Tell children you are going to say two words. Some of the words you say begin with the same sound. Ask them to show you a green counter if the words begin with the same sound. They will show you a red counter if they begin with different sounds. Be sure to stretch out the beginning sound so students can easily hear it.

Oral Riddles

Materials: may want a piece of paper and pencil

Tell students you are going to take sounds away from words to make new words.

"The first word is *gate*."

Tell students the sound you are going to take away from the word.

"If you take away the /g/," then tell students the new word. "you make the word *ate*."

Continue to practice this way until students understand the "game." Then say a word. Ask students to identify the first sound. Tell them to take that sound away and guess what the new word is.

"*Chair*. What is the first sound? /Ch/? If you take /ch/ from *chair* what do you have? *Air*!"

When it is possible, have students draw pictures to go with their riddles. A list of words for adding sounds to make new words is on page 105.

Segmenting the Sounds in a Word - Individual Sounds (Phonemes) (e.g., cat is /c/ /a/ /t/)

Hearing Sounds in Words

Materials: 3-4 counters for each child and several pictures representing words with two sounds (pages 106-108)

Begin with pictures with two sounds, and then progress to three sounds. Show students a picture card. Model how to say each sound in the word (by stretching the word out) and move the counter with it. As a whole group, have students echo the sounds and push the counters after you. As students become better at separating the sounds (stretching them out) have them take turns saying the segmented word individually. After students can successfully separate the sounds individually have each student draw a picture card and share the segmented sounds.

Popcorn

Materials: several three-sound picture cards (pages 103-104)

Show students a picture card. Have the first student on your left stand and say the first sound in the picture then quickly sit down. Move to the next student. Have him stand and say the second sound in the picture and quickly sit down. Have the third student stand and say the last sound and quickly sit down. The sounds and movement should move quickly like popcorn popping.

Blending Sounds to Make Words-Blending the Beginning Sound up to the First Vowel (Onset) and the Rest of the Word (Rime) (e.g., /c/ /at/ is cat)

Beginning and End

Materials: 3-4 counters for each child and several picture cards (pages 100, 102-104, 111-115)

Without showing the picture say the onset and rime in a word.

/h/ /at/

It may be helpful to use counters as you say the word. Have students guess the word. Then show the picture and say the word accurately.

hat

As students become better at the game have students, one at a time, draw a card that no one else can see. That student then shares the segmented sounds of the word. Other players blend the sounds to make a word and guess what the picture is.

Cheers

Materials: several picture cards (pages 100, 102-104, 111-115)

Have each child draw a picture card. When it is their turn they "cheer" the onset and rime of the picture. The other group members return with a cheer of the blended word.

Blending Sounds to Make Words-Individual Sounds (Phonemes) (e.g., /c/ /a/ /t/ is cat)

Putting Sounds Together to Make Words

Materials: several pictures representing words with two or three sounds (pages 102-104)

Without showing the picture to the students say each sound in a word.

/h/ /a/ /t/

Have students guess the word. Show the picture and say the word accurately.

hat

As students become more proficient have students, one at a time, draw a card that no one else can see. That student shares the segmented sounds of the word. Other players blend the sounds to make a word and guess what the picture is.

Oral Riddles

Materials: may want a piece of paper for each student

Tell students you are going to add sounds to words to make new words.

"The first word is *ink*."

Tell students the sound you are going to add to the word.

"If you add /p/ you make the word *pink*."

Continue to practice this way until students understand the "game." Then say a word. Tell students the sound to add. Then ask them to guess what the new word is.

"The word is air. If you add /ch/ to *air* what do you have? *Chair* !"

When it is possible, have students draw pictures to go with their riddles. A list of words for adding sound to make to new words is on page 105.

Substituting Sounds to Make New Words

Oral Riddles

Materials: none

Begin working with words with two sounds, and then three sounds, then four. Say a word.

"The word is *pig*."

Tell students you are going to take away the beginning sound and make it a new sound.

"If you take away the /p/ and add a /b/ you make big."

Continue to practice this way until students understand the "game." Then say a word. Ask students to identify the first sound. Tell them to take that sound away and put another sound in its place then guess what the new word is.

"*Mow*. If you take away the /m/ and add a /s/ what do you have? *Sow*."

"*Sow*. If you take away the /s/ and add a /b/ what do you have? *Bow*."

"*Bow*. If you take away the /b/ and add a /r/ what do you have? *Row*."

A list of words for substituting sounds is on page 106.

How Many Can We Make?

Materials: several counters

Tell students they are going to make some words. You will keep track of how many words they can make. Begin with a word that has several rhymes, such as *bat*. Have children take away the beginning sound and add a new sound. If the new sound makes a word place a counter in the middle of the table. Continue moving from child to child until no new words can be made. Count the counters on the table to determine how many words were made.

Developing Letter and Sound Relationships

Purpose: learn individual letter names and letter sounds

Many children will learn the names and sounds of each of the letters of the alphabet through many reading experiences. Some children will come to school with few reading experiences; others will need more direct instruction before they can learn the letter names and/or sounds. Learning the names and sounds of the letters provides an important foundation for children when they learn to read new words.

It is important that children spend time reading books while they are learning the names and sounds of the letters of the alphabet. This reinforces the sounds being learned and allows the child to practice this new skill.

Suggested Letter and Sound Activities

Letter and Sound Relationships	Activities
Identifying letters	Letters in a Name
	A Little Math
	Read the Room
	Read the Hall and School
	Matching Capital and Lowercase Letters
	The Letter Game
	Letter Bingo
	Letter Tic-Tac-Toe
Matching sounds	Matching Sound to Sound
	Tongue Twisters
Matching sounds and letters	What Sound Is This?
	Alphabet Wall
	Matching Sounds and Letters
	Sound Bingo
	Sound Tic-Tac-Toe

Identifying Letters of the Alphabet

Letters in Names

Materials: Use foam or magnetic letters to help students learn the names of the letters of the alphabet. These allow students to touch the letter and add a tactile mode to the lesson.

My Name

Begin by teaching each student the names of the letters in her name. Touch each letter as you say its name. Have the child touch the letter and echo the letter name after you. When students are successful saying the names of the letters in order then mix the letters up and ask them to say them.

My Friends' Names

After learning the letters in his name teach him the letters in a friend's name. When students are successful saying the names of the letters in a friend's name in order then mix the letters up and ask them to say them.

A Little Math

Materials: a blank Venn Diagram on a sheet of paper for each pair of students

Have students work in pairs to sort the letters of their names by those that are shared and those that are not. Give each pair a Venn Diagram. Begin by laying out all of the letters in each student's name saying the name of the letter as you work. When finished each student should have their name spelled out in front of them.

Have students, one at a time, choose a letter (from either name), and say the name of the letter. If it is a letter in her name she should place it in the circle front of her. If it is a letter in both names she should place it in the middle of the two circles. If it is a letter in her partner's name she should place it in the circle in front of her partner.

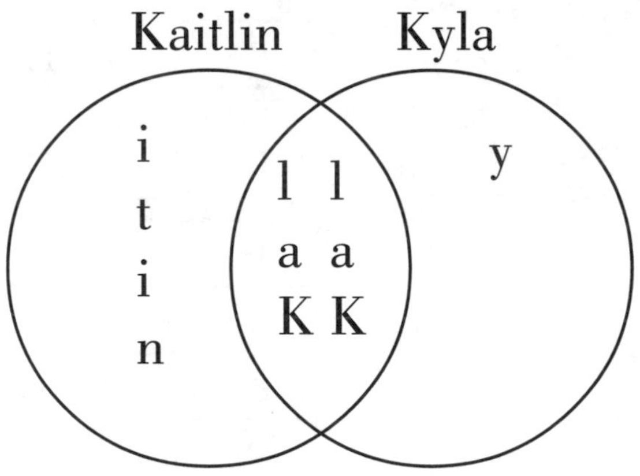

Read the Room

Materials: sentence strips and marker

Once students learn the letter in their name and the letters in their friend's names they are ready to find other things in the room that start with the same letters. Label these things and other objects and features in the room.

Kaitlin

k - kindergarten

i - intercom

a - apple

Erica

e - exit

r - recess

c - computer

Read the Hall and School

Materials: sentence strips and marker

Find other things in the hall and school that start with these letters. Label these things.

Kaitlin

k - kite

a - alphabet

c - cat

Erica

e - enter

r - radio

i - icicle

Matching Capital and Lowercase Letters

Materials: deck of cards with capital and lowercase letters

Pass out four cards to each player. Players place the four cards face up on the table in front of them. The first player selects one of her letter cards, capital or lowercase, to match to another player's capital or lowercase letter card. To complete the match she must name the letters. If she can make a match she takes the two cards and places them beside her and the next player takes a turn. If she can't make a match she draws from the pile. If she can then make a match she places the match beside her. If not the new card is placed face up with her other cards. The object of the game is the match all of the cards on the table. There are no "winners."

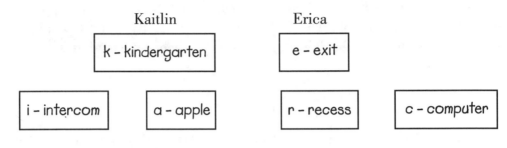

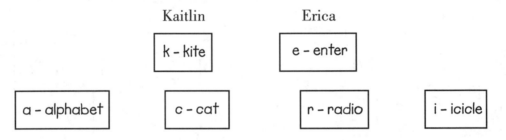

The Letter Game

Materials: Letter Game game board, letter cards, and die (pages 108-109, 123), place markers

Have each player roll the die. The player with the highest number moves first. The player moves the number of letters on the die. When she is done moving she must say the name of the letter she lands on. If she says the correct letter, she stays there. If she doesn't, she moves back to the square she started from. The players become "advisors" as they reach the mailbox. If remaining players need assistance they may ask one of the advisors. The advisors may not give advice or information until a player asks them for help. The game is over when all players have reached the mailbox.

Letter Bingo

Materials: a Bingo card for each student (page 110)

The instructor can make the card with the letters being studied or students can make their own Bingo cards with the letters they know. If students make their own Bingo cards have them write the letters they used on a small piece of paper so you will have letters to draw. Call out letters and have students mark that letter on their cards. The first person to cover all of the letters (blackout) on their card gets to call the letters next game.

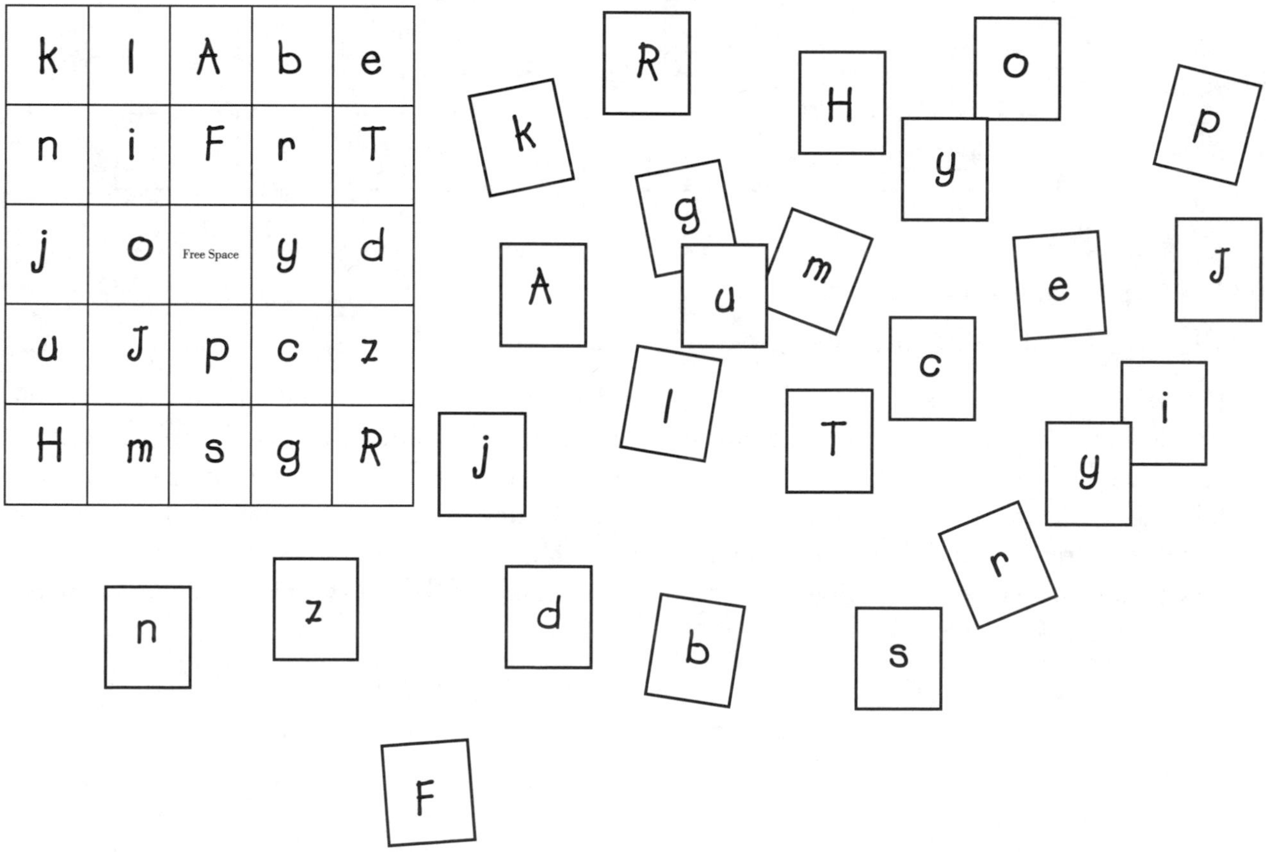

Letter Tic-Tac-Toe

Note: In order for this game to be successful students must know how to play Tic-Tac-Toe.

Materials: Tic-Tac-Toe card (page 107) for each pair of students

Place students in pairs. Give each pair a Tic-Tac-Toe card. You can make the card with the letters you have been studying or each student can make a Tic-Tac-Toe card with letters they know. If students make their own cards they will play two games with their partner—one with their card and one with their partner's card.

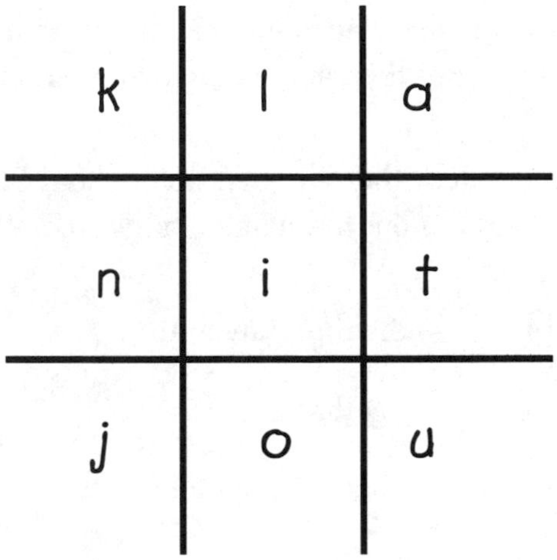

Have students call out the letter they want to mark.

i

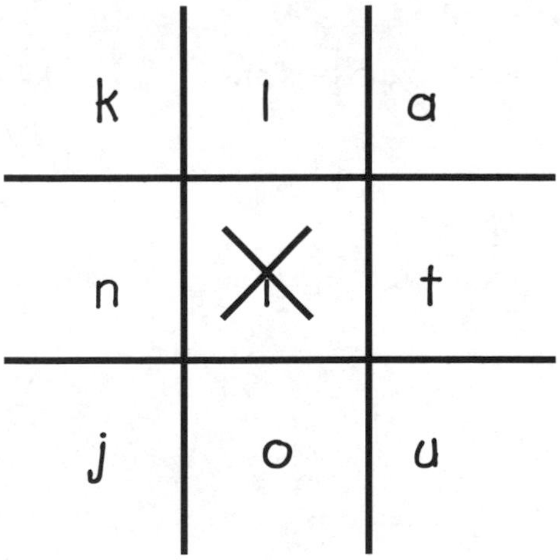

u

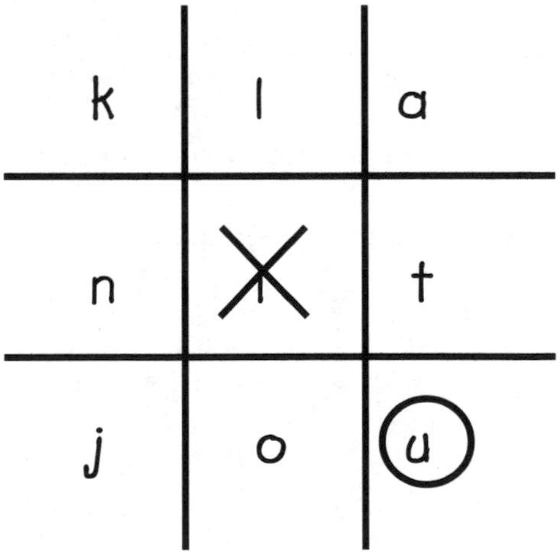

The first person to get three in a row on his card gets to start the next game. If it's a "Cat's Game" the other player gets to start the next game.

Matching Sounds

Matching Sound to Sound

Materials: Make or purchase a set of cards with a picture on one side and the corresponding letter on the other (pictures with beginning sounds represented are on pages 111-115). Be sure to work on consonant sounds only.

Pass out four cards to each player. Players place the four cards face up on the table in front of them. The first player selects one of her cards to match to another player's card. To make the match she must find two pictures that begin with the same sound. If she can make a match she takes the two cards and places them beside her and the next player takes a turn. If she can't make a match she draws from the pile. If she can then make a match she places the match beside her. If not, the new card is placed face up with her other cards. The object of the game is the match all of the cards on the table—there are no "winners."

If a child has trouble finding a match, then the instructor should carefully stretch out the beginning sound of the chosen card then stretch out the name of all of the other cards and ask if it is a match.

- /k/ kangaroo /t/ table Is that a match?
- /k/ kangaroo /s/ sun Is that a match?
- /k/ kangaroo /k/ kitchen Is that a match?

Tongue Twisters

Materials: tongue twisters from books or word plays (a list of tongue twister books is on page 126)

Choose a tongue twister that highlights one of the letters of the alphabet students have been practicing. Have students read it several times.

Karl Kessler kept the ketchup in the kitchen.

Then choose the name of a student (or students) to create a new tongue twister.

Karen and Keith keep a kangaroo in kindergarten.

Have students illustrate the tongue twister for Karen and Keith.

Matching Sounds and Letters

What Sound Is This?

Materials: none

Begin by isolating the beginning sounds of the children's' names and telling students the name of the letter that makes that sound. This is the same concept as stretching the sounds, segmenting the first sound from the rest of the name.

- Kaitlin /k/ k says /k/
- Erica /e/ e says /ĕ/
- Tabitha /t/ t says /t/

Then isolate the beginning consonant sounds of the labeled items in the room.

- table /t/ t says /t/
- computer /c/ c says /c/

After modeling the activity several times have students tell you the name of the letter when you segment the beginning sound of a name or an object in the room. Then provide students with a sound and have them identify items in the room that begin with that sound.

Alphabet Wall

Materials: letters of the alphabet, large wall space, or chart paper

Identify a space on the wall to display with all of the letters of the alphabet. If you don't have a room that allows for this, use a large sheet of chart paper that can be rolled up and used each time the group meets. Allow children to place the names of things under each letter:

- students' names
- labels for things in the classroom
- pictures from favorite books
- student-drawn pictures

Matching Sounds and Letters

Materials: Make or purchase a set of cards with the picture on one side and the corresponding letter on the other (pictures for making sound and letter cards can be found on pages 100, 102-104, 111-115).

Pass out four cards to each player. Players place the four cards face up on the table in front of them. The first player selects one of her cards to match to another player's card. To make the match she must find two pictures that begin with the same sound and be able to identify the name of the letter that makes the sound. If she can make a match she takes the two cards and places them beside her and the next player takes a turn. If she can't make a match she draws from the pile. If she can then make a match she places the match beside her. If not, the new card is placed face up with her other cards. The object of the game is to match all of the cards on the table—there are no "winners."

If a child has trouble finding a match then the instructor should carefully stretch out the beginning sound of the chosen card then stretch out the name of all of the other cards and ask if it is a match

- /k/ kangaroo   /t/ table   Is that a match?
- /k/ kangaroo   /s/ sun   Is that a match?
- /k/ kangaroo   /k/ kitchen   Is that a match?

Sound Bingo

Materials: a Bingo card (page 110)

You can make the card with the letters you have been studying or students can make their own Bingo cards with the letters they know. If students make their own Bingo cards, have them place the letters they used on a small piece of paper so you will have letters to draw. Call out letters. If students have that letter on their card, they may only mark the letter after they say the sound of the letter. The first person to cover all of the letters on their card (blackout) gets to call the letters next game.

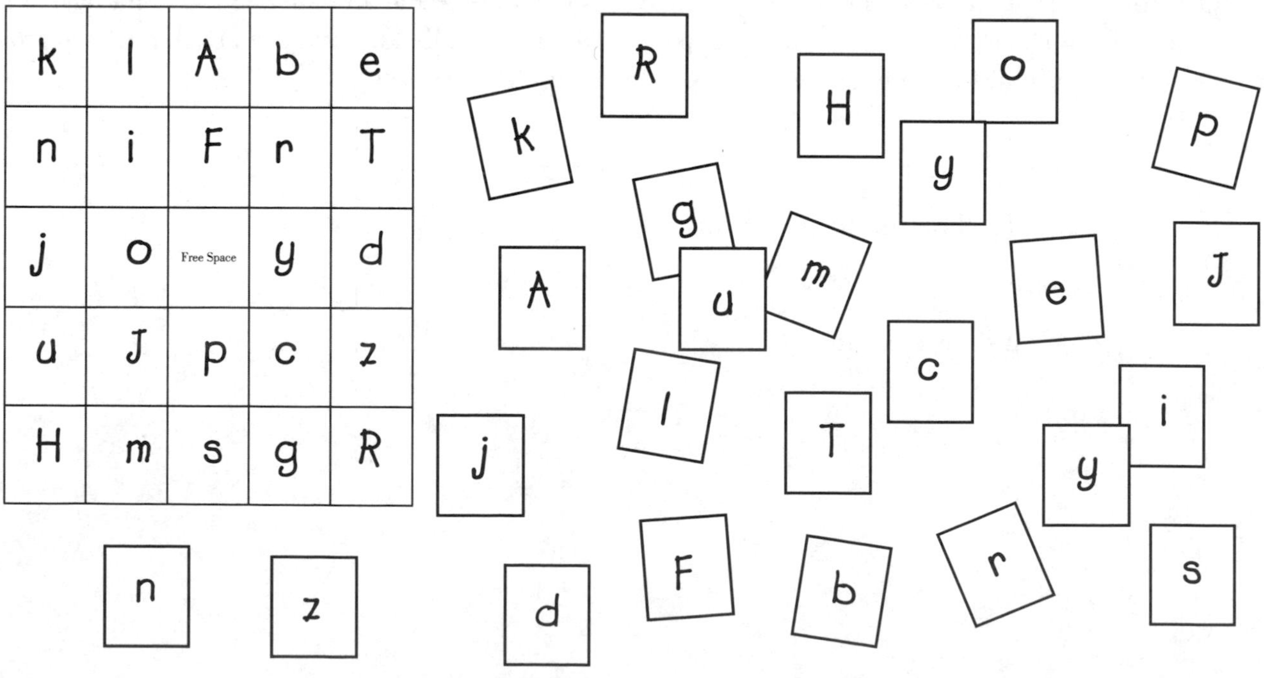

Sound Tic-Tac-Toe

Materials: piece of paper with a Tic-Tac-Toe card (page 107) for each pair of students

Place students in pairs. Give each pair a Tic-Tac-Toe card. You can make the card with the letters you have been studying or each student can make a Tic-Tac-Toe card with letters they know. If students make their own cards they will play two games with their partner—one with their card and one with their partner's card. Have students call out the name and sound of the letter they want to mark. The first person to get three in a row on her card gets to start the next game. If it's a "Cat's Game" the other player gets to start the next game.

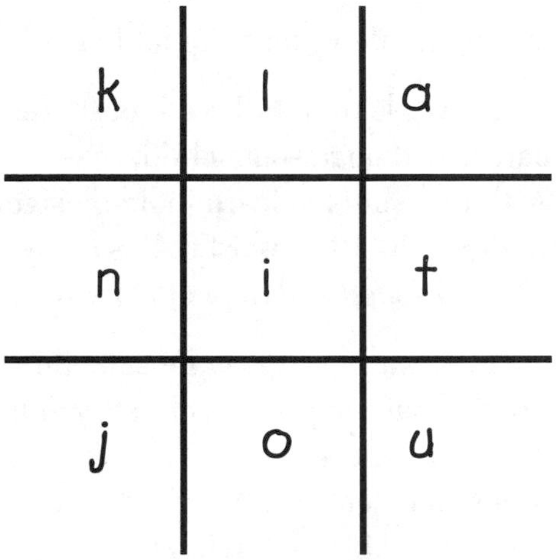

l /l/

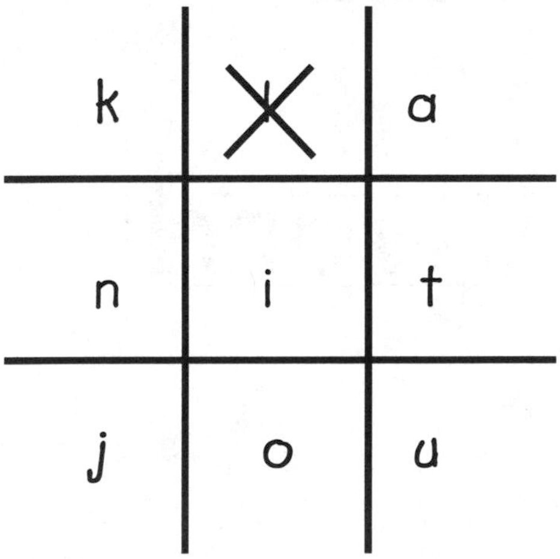

j /j/

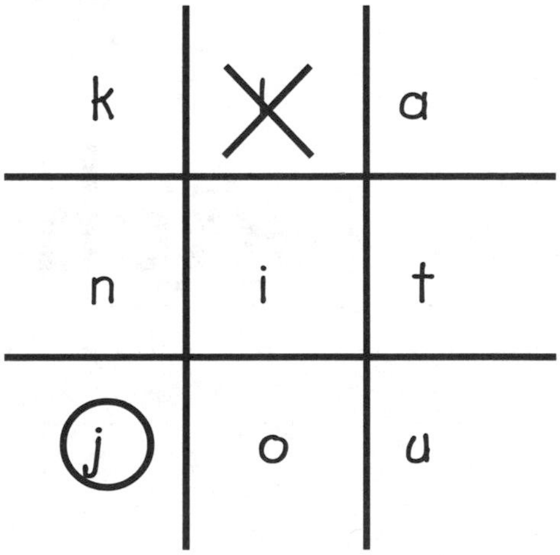

Chapter Four

Learning Words

While children are developing phonemic awareness skills and learning the names and sounds of the letters of the alphabet, they are also ready to learn some words. Some words children will need to learn by sight. Others they will be able to read by learning some decoding strategies.

Learning Sight Words

Purpose: To learn high frequency words so that they can be quickly read by sight.

Students need to become familiar with the words they will read most often in stories. The most common way for sight words to be taught is with flash cards. Although some children will be successful working with flash cards, most children need more experience with the words to learn them by sight. Instead of flash cards have students work with words on a word wall (Cunningham, 2000). A word wall is a physical location for commonly read words. Word wall words should be practiced daily through a variety of activities.

The physical space for a word wall may be a wall, or it may be something more portable. If the words are to be attached to a wall, there needs to be enough space to place each letter of the alphabet in order with enough space under each letter to place several words. Some letters need more space than others (e.g., there are many more "w" sight words than "v" sight words). Words placed on walls are written large enough so all children can see them. The words are outlined so the shape of each word is highlighted.

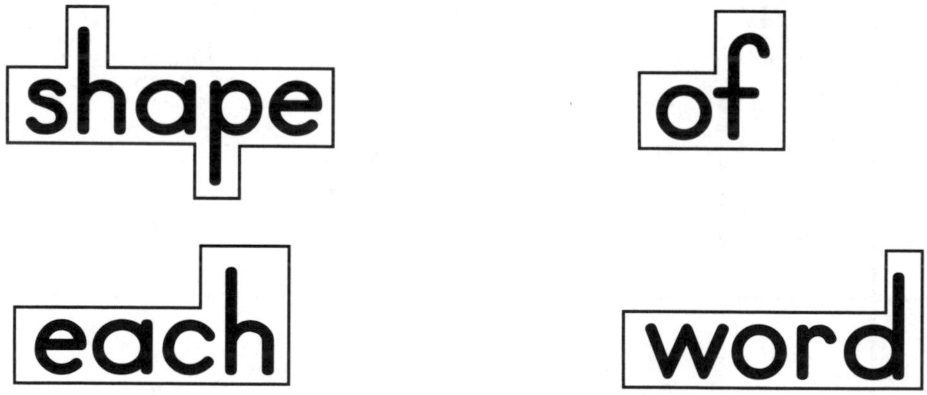

Portable Word Wall

If wall space is not available, there are two ways to create portable word walls: with file folders or chart paper. File folder word walls are created for each student. The folders have the letters of the alphabet written across both sides. The student or the instructor writes new words under each letter as they are introduced. Words are outlined so the shape of each word is highlighted.

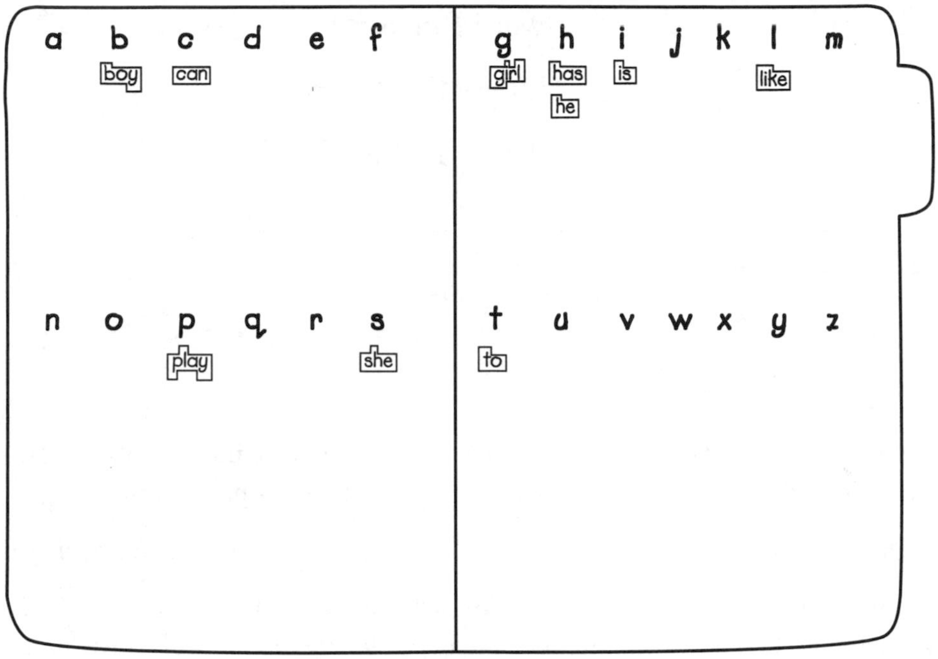

Another alternative is to keep the word wall on a piece of chart paper that can be displayed each time the group meets. New words are added as they are introduced.

Depending upon the grade level placement and the reading level of the child she may work with a word wall in the classroom with grade level words and have an individual word wall folder that has the list of words at her instructional reading level.

It is also helpful to write the word wall words on index-size cards for each child. This way they can manipulate the words while practicing and playing games.

All children in the group work with the same list of words. Two to five new words are introduced each week. Children should work with Word Wall and On the Back Activities for at least five minutes daily. The other word games may be played in the time remaining for this segment of the session.

Suggested Learning Words Activities

Word Wall

On the Back Activities

Word Bird

Word Bingo

Interactive Charts

Word Tic-Tac-Toe

Word Wall

Materials to make a word wall: a dedicated wall with space for approximately 50 words, sentence strips, index cards; or a file folder for each student, index cards; or a piece of chart paper, index cards

Materials to "do" the daily word wall activities: half sheet of paper and pencil for each child

On the first day introduce the two to five new words, one at a time. Give each student a half sheet of paper and a pencil. Have students number the paper for the number of words that are to be introduced.

To introduce a word:

- Point to the word and read it aloud.
- Use it in a sentence.
- Read it again.
- Students then clap, chant, or cheer each letter then say the word.
- Students write the word on a half sheet of paper.
- After all words are written, have students edit each word by placing their pencils under each letter in a word as it is said by the instructor.
- Finally, have students trace the shape of each word.

The next day the new words are reviewed following the same routine (read, use in sentence, read, clap, write, edit, trace shape).

New words are introduced every three to five sessions. Any three to five words from the word wall are selected for review for session three, four, or five. You might want to select words children have a difficult time with or words that are easily confused. These may be words that begin with the same letter, have similar shapes, etc. The same routine is followed with these words.

On the Back Activities

After children have practiced the new words or the review words have them turn the paper over and do another kind of review with the words. You may want to select one of the following review activities suggested by Cunningham, Hall, and Sigmon (1999) in *The Teacher's Guide to the Four Blocks®*:

- Write all of the words on the wall that start with a particular sound.
- Write all of the rhyming words.
- Write all of the words that have three sounds.
- Write all of the words that fit in a sentence (provided by the instructor).

    We can ____ outside.

- Play "Be a Mind Reader."

    This is a fun way for students to review words and to practice listening.

    1. Students number the paper one to five.
    2. The instructor gives five clues.
    3. The first clue is always "It's one of the words on the wall."
    4. Students choose any word to write on line one.
    5. The instructor gives another clue. The clue should include features that students have been practicing (beginning sound, number of letters, rhymes with..., number of sounds, etc.).
    6. Students either write the word they already chose again on line two or choose another word. The goal is to continuously match the word they are writing with all of the clues given so far.
    7. The instructor continues to give clues.
    8. After clue five all children read their word.

Mind Reader Clues for *Go*
It's one of the words on the wall.
It has two letters.
It rhymes with toe.
It starts with the letter g.
It ends the sentence, "I want to ___".

Word Bird

Materials: Word Bird game board, word cards, die (pages 116-123), place markers

Have each player roll the die. The player with the highest number moves first. The player moves the number on the die. When he is done moving he must draw a word card and read the word correctly. Encourage him to use the word wall to help him read the word. If he reads it correctly he stays there. If he is incorrect, he must go back to where he started.

Players become "advisors" once they reach Word Bird. Remaining players may ask the advisors for clues. Advisors may give the player a sentence with the word missing or tell the player a word that rhymes with it. The game is over when all players have reached the reading Word Bird.

Note: You may choose to make sentence cards with the high-frequency words in them rather than use the words cards provided. Players would have to read the sentence to move to the next space.

Word Bingo

Materials: Bingo card for each student (page 110)

Give each student a Bingo card. You can make the card with the words you have been studying or students can make their own Bingo cards with the words they know. If students make their own Bingo cards have them write the words they used on a small piece of paper so you will have words to draw. Call out words and have students mark that word on their cards. The first person to cover all of the words on their card (blackout) gets to call the words next game.

to	go	a	like	me
I	will	not	be	dog
cat	boy	Free Space	big	who
you	what	on	in	is
has	can	day	do	are

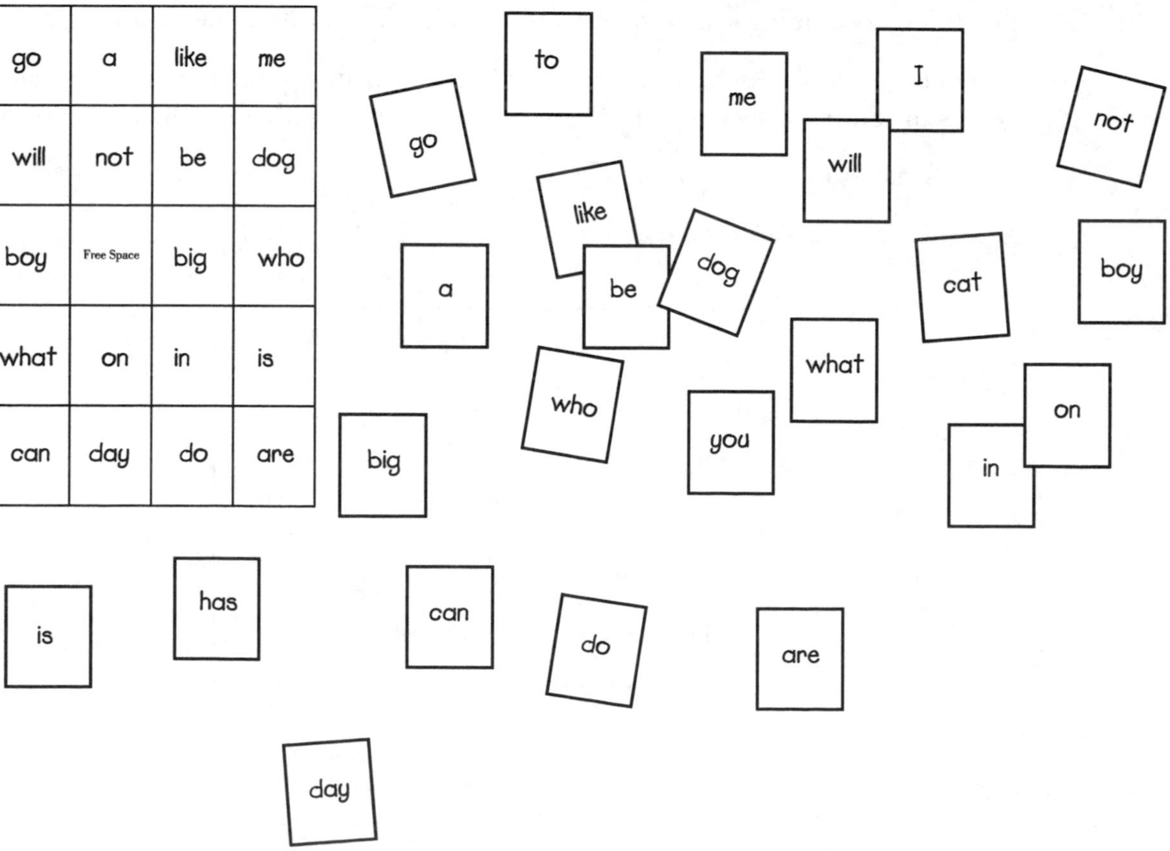

Interactive Charts

Materials: interactive chart and word cards

Interactive charts are charts that allow children to read a familiar text such as a nursery rhyme, poem, finger play, or song and manipulate one word or phrase. Reading an interactive chart provides an opportunity for children to transfer their oral language skills to written language. It is a way for children to learn commonly seen words such as color words, number words, and animal names. It is most helpful to use student names whenever possible.

> Jack be nimble; Jack be quick.
> Jack jump over the candlestick.

During subsequent readings, use word cards with the names of your students instead of Jack.

> Kaitlin be nimble; Kaitlin be quick.
> Kaitlin jump over the candlestick.

Number and counting rhymes make great interactive charts. After reading "Six in the Bed" with the children, change the number word from six to five, then read the new verse together.

> Six in the Bed
> There were six in the bed
> And the little one said,
> "Roll over. Roll over."
> So they all rolled over
> And one fell out.

> Six in the Bed
> There were five in the bed
> And the little one said,
> "Roll over. Roll over."
> So they all rolled over
> And one fell out.

Continue changing the number word and reading the new verse until there is no one left to fall out.

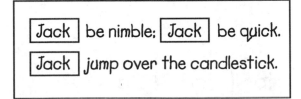

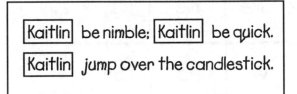

Word Tic-Tac-Toe

Materials: Tic-Tac-Toe card (page 107) for each pair of students

Place students in pairs. Give each pair a Tic-Tac-Toe card. You can make the card with the words you have been studying or each student can make a Tic-Tac-Toe card with words they know. If students make their own cards they will play two games with their partner—one with their card and one with their partner's card. Have students call out the word they want to mark. They must then use it in a sentence. The first person to get three in a row on his card gets to start the next game. If it's a "Cat's Game" the other player gets to start the next game.

to	go	a
like	me	I
will	not	be

me

I like me.

to	go	a
like	~~me~~	I
will	not	be

be

I want to be an artist.

to	go	a
like	~~me~~	I
will	not	be

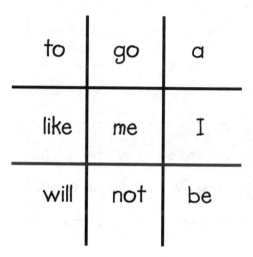

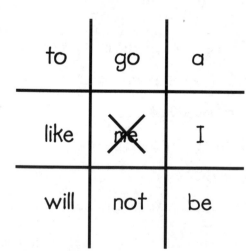

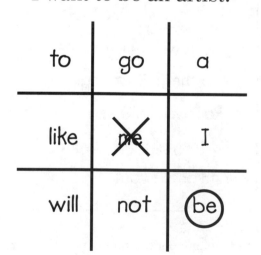

Decoding New Words

Purpose: To learn strategies that help in reading unfamiliar words.

Activities for decoding new words are Guess the Covered Word, Making Words, Guess a Letter, and Word Wheels. These activities may be done once or twice a week for variety.

Guess the Covered Word

Guess the Covered Word lessons, introduced in the *Teacher's Guide to the Four-Blocks* (Cunningham, Hall, and Sigmon, 1999), require students to use all of the information good readers use as they try to figure out a missing word from a sentence. Good readers ask three questions as they try to decode an unfamiliar word. As they select a word to complete the sentence they ask:

- Does the word make sense?
- Is the word the right shape and size?
- Does the word begin with the right sound?

Materials: overhead transparency or chart paper, sticky notes

Write three to five sentences on a piece of chart paper or on an overhead transparency. One word in the sentence will be covered so students will have to guess what it is. Some suggestions for the first few times this activity is done:

- Write sentences with the covered word at the end of the sentence.
- Make the covered word a word with a single beginning consonant.
- Use students' names in the sentences.

Chad likes his <u>dog</u>.
Amy is a good <u>reader</u>.
Angie wants to play <u>catch</u>.
Kyla likes to eat <u>bananas</u>.

Place sticky notes over the word in the sentence that students are to decode. Two sticky notes are used: the first covers the word from beginning letter to the first vowel; the second covers the word from the first vowel to the end of the word. Each sticky note should be cut to match the shape of the covered word.

Chad likes his dog.
Chad likes his dog.

Show only the first sentence to students and ask them to guess the covered word. You write the students' best guesses on the chalkboard.

After hearing from several students look at the words and tell students they will need to answer some questions about each word to see if they are correct. Post the following sentences for students to see:

1. Does this word make sense?
2. Is the word the right shape and size?

   Say each word and then ask students to think about each question. After discussing the word and questions cross off any word that does not make sense or is the wrong shape.

   Look at all remaining words. Tell students there is one more question that needs to be answered.

3. Does it begin with the right sound?

   To answer this question you will need to remove the first sticky note showing the beginning sound. Have students look at the remaining words. If none of them begin with that sound take a few more suggestions, reminding students that the words they give must make sense, be the correct shape, and begin with that sound.

Uncover the word completely and read the sentence. Then begin the same activity with the next sentence.

As students become better at guessing the covered word at the end of the sentence try the following:

- Move the word to the middle of the sentence.
- Make the sentences into a paragraph with more complex ideas.

You can purchase Guess the Covered Word activity books with sentences and transparencies already created. These are graded resources, e.g., *Guess the Covered Word for First Grade*, *Guess the Covered Word for Second Grade*, and *Guess the Covered Word for Third Grade* (see the list of Professional Resources on pages 125-126). You will want to choose the book that is the average reading level of the students you are working with. This will most likely not be at their grade level.

Making Words

This activity, just as the name says, has students make words from a given set of letters.

Materials: each student needs a particular set of letters of the alphabet, a set of letters for the pocket chart, word cards (on an index card), pocket chart

You may choose to make a set of the letters of the alphabet for each child to have, or you may choose to provide children with strips of letters they will need for each Making Words activity. If you choose to make an alphabet set for children you may want to make the vowels a different color to easily identify them. You will also need to decide how you want to store them and make them available to children.

a	b	c	d	e	f	g	h	i	j
k	l	m	n	o	p	q	r	s	t
u	v	w	x	y	z				

If you choose to provide children with strips of letters for each lesson, they will need scissors to cut them apart.

a	i	n	s	t

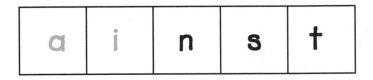

To prepare for a making words activity you must first decide which words children will be making. You will need to make those letters available to students. You will also need to write the words to be made on index cards for students to see.

The best resource for working with small groups of children reading below grade level is *Systematic Sequential Phonics They Use* by Pat Cunningham (2000). This book has 140 short, focused making words lessons that develop word wall words. It is intended for instructors working with Title One or other special needs students. You can also purchase the *Month-by-Month Phonics* book series by Patricia Cunningham and Dorothy Hall (1998). These books are filled with "big" words and all of the little words that can be made with those letters words.

Making Word Wall Words

Tell children that they will be building some of the words from the word wall with the letters you give them. Decide which words on the wall you will want them to make. Give them enough letters to make four or five of the words on the word wall. Decide if there are other words that can be made from those letters. Write those words and the word wall words on index cards.

Tell students the first word they are to make with the letters. Then use the word in a sentence.

in   My lunch is *in* my lunch box.

Watch as children make the word. Choose one student to make the word correctly with letters in the pocket chart. Don't worry about all of the children having the word spelled correctly before asking someone to build it in the pocket chart. Seeing the correct spelling in the pocket chart will help the others make the word.

Once the word is spelled correctly place an index card with the word written on it in the pocket chart. Remove the letters used to spell the word and continue to give students words to make from the available letters.

in   at   is   as   it   an

Now tell children they are going to make some words with the letters that are not on the word wall. These words have word wall words in them.

tan   sat   sit

Again, show children the words on cards in the pocket chart.

When all of the words are spelled sort them by:

- beginning letter(s)
- word endings
- rhyming words

Making Secret Words

Tell children they are still making words, but some of these will not be on the word wall. When they are done making these words they will use all of the letters to make a secret word. For example, if you gave students the letters *a*, *i*, *n*, and *r* you would teach the following lesson.

Tell students the word they are to make with the letters. Then use the word in a sentence.

in My lunch is *in* my lunch box.

Watch as children make the word. Choose one student to make the word correctly with letters in the pocket chart. Continue to give students words to make from the available letters.

in an ran air

Select the order in which the words are made so they are made by changing only one or two letters at a time. You might say something like, "Find two letters to spell the word *in*. My lunch is *in* my lunch box."

Continue to give students words to make from the available letters. "Change one letter to make the word *an*. I am *an* adult. Add one letter to make *ran*. I *ran* home from school. Change one letter and rearrange the letters to make *air*. I hope the *air* is clean."

Tell students they are ready to use all of the letters to make the secret word: *rain*.

When all of the words are spelled sort them by:

- beginning letter(s)
- word endings
- rhyming words

Now have students make new words with the words on the index cards by adding other letters. Ask them to tell you how to make the words:

fin rang can pair

You write their responses on the chalkboard and on an index card, then place the written word in the pocket chart.

Guess a Letter

This activity, played like Hangman, encourages children to attend to all of the letters in the word.

Materials: Word Wall

Select a word from the Word Wall to be guessed. You may want to use one of the more difficult or confusing Word Wall words. Write a blank on the chalkboard for each letter. Prepare a clue for students to help them think about the word to be guessed.

___ ___ ___ ___ ___ ___ Clue: Someone you like.

The first child makes a letter guess. If the letter is correct write the letter on each blank that it fits. This child does not make another guess; the turn passes to the next child.

___ ___ ___ e ___ ___

If the guess is wrong the letter is written in a box off to the side, and the next child takes a turn.

___ ___ ___ e ___ ___ [g]

No one may guess the word until all letters are completed. The child to guess the last letter gets to read first. If they are unsuccessful the turn passes to the next child.

f r i e n d [g s u]

The winner is the child who correctly reads the word. This child gets to write the letters on the board for the next game. If this child has already had a turn then they may choose someone who has not had a turn.

Word Wheels

Materials: poster board, 9" paper plates, brads, paper squares, tape rolls, copy of Word Wheel for each student (page 128)

Cut the poster board into 9" circles. Glue a copy of the Word Wheel from page 128 onto the circle. Cut a square out of the paper plate to match the Word Wheel pattern. Give each student a poster board circle, a paper plate and a brad. Show them how to assemble the wheel.

Tell students to write a word ending on a piece of paper and tape it to the paper plate. (e.g., -at)

Turn the Word Wheel letter by letter to see what words can be made. Have students keep a list of words made with the ending. Have students identify that these words rhyme.

Vocabulary

Chapter Five

As students continue to develop their reading skills they will encounter words that are more difficult to understand and decode. Traditionally teachers have had students look up words in the dictionary, write words in sentences, or memorize word meanings. These activities do not have a long-term effect on vocabulary development (Pennsylvania Department of Education, 2001). To maximize vocabulary development it will be important to identify what words need to be learned and select an activity or activities that allow the students to be actively involved in the learning process.

Choosing Words to Teach

Research has found that it is not necessary to know every word in a passage in order to understand it. It has also been found that teaching all new words in a passage will not necessarily increase the reader's understanding of the passage. It is recommended that teachers choose only a few words to teach. To determine which new words to introduce during vocabulary instruction you should:

- Teach words that are essential to understanding a passage.

  You can decide if the word is essential by asking, "If readers do not know the meaning of this word, will they still be able to understand the passage?" Often, new words are not related to the main idea or an important detail, and they would not affect the meaning of the story if they weren't learned. Choose only those words that are directly related to the passage's main ideas or concepts.

- Teach common words or words that are generally useful for students to know.

  Students should become familiar with certain words because they will see those words in the future.

Once the important vocabulary words have been selected, instructors need to choose activities that will introduce the words to students. Some ideas that make a difference in children learning new vocabulary are:

- Read to and have children read a lot.

  Children will learn most vocabulary words by reading and/or being read to. This does not mean that instructors shouldn't teach some vocabulary words. The best vocabulary development is a result of reading and teaching word meanings.

- Activities should actively involve students with the new words.

  Students need to read, hear, write, and speak the new vocabulary word so that the word becomes part of their everyday vocabularies.

The following activities—Word Webs, Word Sorts, and Rivet—will support students as they learn to decode and understand new words. The activities work with words that are increasingly more difficult. The last two may be more appropriate for older children.

Word Webs

Word Webs are a visual display of words that are related to one another.

Materials: chalkboard or chart paper

First identify the main idea of the story. Then select several vocabulary words that are directly related to the main idea and may be new to students. Draw a large oval and place a word (or phrase) that represents the main idea from the story. If you were working with the story, *Can I Keep Him?* by Steven Kellogg, you might start with the main idea animals.

Write one of the vocabulary words to the side of the oval. In this story, the first animal introduced is a dog.

Think aloud about the vocabulary word and how it is related to the concept. "I know that animals are living things that move around. There are lots of different kinds of animals. Some animals are pets. Pets are animals that live with people. One kind of pet is a dog."

Draw a box or oval around the word and then connect them with lines or arrows to the main idea.

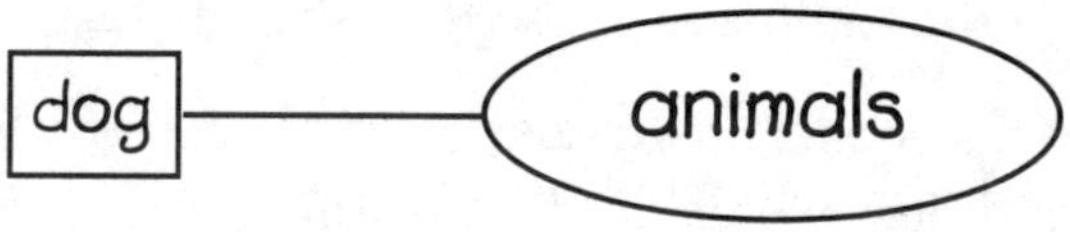

The out-loud conversation you have with yourself as you write the words and draw the connections is the most important part of the lesson.

"Another kind of pet is a kitten. I can show that dogs and kittens are pets by connecting them with and arrow and writing the word *pets*."

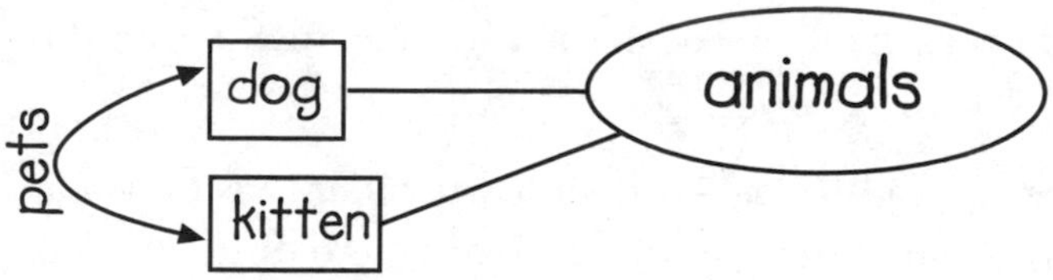

"Kittens are baby cats. I can show that they are cats by drawing an arrow down from *kitten* and writing *cats*."

Continue to introduce the vocabulary from the story as you talk and show the relationships.

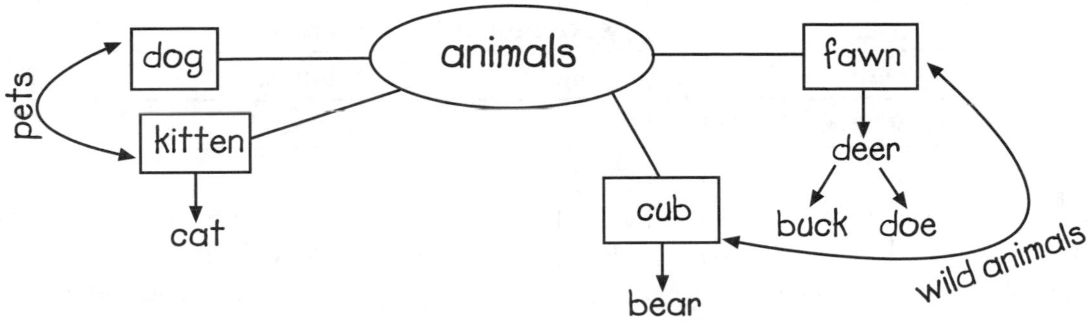

Once students are familiar with the mapping process they may work in groups to brainstorm as many words as they can think of that are related to the main idea of a book. The instructor then makes a class word map using each group's results. Again, the instructor thinks aloud focusing students' attention on the vocabulary words and their connections to the main idea. It will be necessary for the instructor to add any vocabulary from the story she thinks is important that students do not come up with in their brainstorming.

Word Sorts

Materials: index cards

Provide students with lists of words previously discussed in class. Have them work with partners or in a group to sort the words into groups or categories.

There are two kinds of sorting that can be done: closed sorts and open sorts.

"Closed Sorts" are sorting activities with predetermined categories. In a closed sort the instructor would provide the category labels and have students place each word into one category. For example: vocabulary words from the story *Titch* by Pat Hutchins might be categorized by size, toys, instruments, and tools.

size	toys	instruments	tools
little	great big bike	drum	saw
a bit bigger	big bike	trumpet	hammer
a lot bigger	tricycle	wooden whistle	nails
	kite		spade
	pinwheel		

"Open Sorts" are sorting activities that require students to create and discuss their own categories. For example, words from stories about woodland animals might be sorted into three categories.

fur	feathers	insects
fox	woodpecker	crickets
bear	owl	beetles
squirrel	crow	ants

Students may also generate their own words for a closed sort or an open sort. Student generated words is a great way to end a topical study. This will assess how well students learned the vocabulary from the study. For example, at the end of a unit on weather students may generate and sort words such as:

wet	frozen	clear
rain	sleet	sunny
drizzle	snow	breezy
	ice	

Rivet

Rivet, developed by Pat Cunningham (2000), is a vocabulary activity that activates children's prior knowledge and gets them to make predictions. It was created so that children will be "riveted" to the board as the vocabulary words are introduced. For additional information on Rivet see *Phonics They Use* (Cunningham, 2000).

Materials: chalkboard or chart paper

Choose several key vocabulary words from the story. Draw enough blanks (like hangman) for every letter in each word. Tell the students that these are words from a story (e.g., *Wagon Wheels* by Barbara Brenner).

___ ___ ___ ___ ___ ___ ___ ___

Fill in the letters to the first word one at a time. Unlike hangman students are not guessing the letters. The instructor fills them in. As letters are being placed, students are encouraged to guess the word at any point.

b r o ___ ___ ___ ___ ___

When someone guesses the correct word have that student help spell it and write the remaining letters on the board.

b r o t h e r s

Repeat the steps for each of the vocabulary words.

b r o t h e r s

t r a v e l

f a r m e r

s e t t l e m e n t

w a g o n

After guessing all of the words have students look at the list and predict what the story may be about. Encourage students to consider several different possibilities. It may be necessary to discuss the meaning of some of the words before taking any guesses.

settlement–a place where people settle to live

"Brothers travel on a wagon to see a farmer on a *settlement*."

"A farmer uses a wagon to take brothers to a *settlement*."

"A farmer from a *settlement* travels with some brothers to buy a wagon."

Leave the predictions posted so children can check them as they read the story.

Most struggling readers will not encounter big (multisyllabic) words in their daily reading or writing. If you think your students would benefit from some instruction in vocabulary strategies to identify and define big words, three such strategies can be found in *Phonics They Use* (Cunningham, 2000). The three suggested strategies are Collecting Big Words, Chunking a Big Word, and Word Detectives.

Chapter Six

Writing

Writing to, with, and by Children

Just as students need many opportunities to be read to, be read with, and read by themselves, they also need opportunities to be written to, written with, and write by themselves. Children should spend some time each day engaged in each activity. The child's writing skills and writing level may determine the amount of time you spend writing to or with children or the amount of time they write by themselves.

You will spend more time writing to children with few print concepts and little knowledge of the alphabet. You will spend some time writing to children with few letter identification and letter/sound relationships and little writing experience. You will spend less time writing to children with letter/sound relationships and more writing experience.

All children will benefit from you writing with them. These writing activities may include messages, stories, journal entries, or charts. More time will be spent writing with children with reading difficulties than those without.

Children should write on their own for a portion of the day each day. This allows children an opportunity to apply what they have learned about print concepts and letters and sounds. If you are pushing in (working with a student or group of students in the context of the classroom), you can reinforce children writing by themselves by being available to assist and/or answer questions.

One thing students will want you to help them with is spelling. Even young children have a sense of correct spelling and often rely on adults to spell words for them. If you provide accurate spelling for all of the words they want to write, they will not learn strategies to support them when you are not available. Often, children with outside support limit the words they write and simply quit when help is not there. Instead, teach students to look around the room for support. They may use the word wall, calendar, topical word lists, or any other words in the room.

For any word that they can't find around the room, students should say the word slowly stretching out the sounds, listen for the sounds they know, and then write the letters that go with those sounds. This allows them to apply what they have learned about letters and sounds. If they aren't sure that the word is spelled correctly, they can circle the word. This reminds them that they need to check it later. Circling the word "frees" the child to continue writing without worrying about correct spelling.

Writing to Children

The writing done to children should be short and focused. It may be an opening message, as you begin the small group work, or a closing message summarizing what was accomplished today. The purpose of the writing is to model how to get ideas down on paper and how to reread what was written. Take time to model what you are thinking (content), how you decided how to make certain words (spelling) including making mistakes and circling them, and how to think about using capital letters and punctuation. Talking out loud as you make these decisions allows the students to listen as you think. This externalizes the thinking process of writing and allows them to better understand what writers do while writing.

Writing with Children

After writing to children for several weeks or sessions, they can participate in the thinking process. Ask them to help you decide what to write, how to make words, and how to decide where to put capital letters and punctuation. Encourage them to (nicely) correct you when you make mistakes. Children can also participate in other writing activities with you.

Writing by Children

Once children understand the mechanics of writing, they are ready to do some writing on their own. Initial writing attempts will be short and difficult to read. You may be more successful asking them to read their writing to you. Do not be concerned with correcting their writing. If you correct their writing, you send the message that it is "wrong," and many children will not attempt to write again. Most children will be able to read their own writing but will be unable to read the corrected writing. There will be opportunities to correct writing later. At first, we are just working on fluency and getting ideas on paper.

Writing to Children

Messages

Materials: chalkboard or chart paper

Begin each session with a two or three sentence message. The message may be about anything:

- telling them what they will be doing today
- reviewing what was done yesterday
- sharing important events in the news
- discussing upcoming school events

The topic of the writing is not important. The out-loud thinking about what you are writing and how you are writing it is the most important aspect of the message.

Your message should not take more than five minutes to write. Limit your message to two or three sentences.

Different Kinds of Writing

Materials: chalkboard or chart paper

Explain to students that there are many different kinds of stories to tell. Not all of them are imaginative. Some describe, some try to get others to agree with the author about something, and some give directions.

Note: There are many different kinds of writing. Here is a description of four different styles:

A *narrative writing* tells a story. The story should have a beginning, middle, and end that may be all contained in one paragraph or several. A narrative writing should describe the "five W's" (who, what, where, when, why) with many colorful details. As a model you may choose to write about a favorite childhood memory or a historical event. This is the writing students most often attempt to create. If they have difficulty with writing, you may suggest they try another kind of writing.

A *descriptive writing* describes a person, place, thing, or idea. You may choose to describe the members of your family, a favorite vacation spot, or a pet. In your writing be sure to model the use of describing words to draw a mental picture of your topic.

An *expository writing* gives directions, tells how to do something, or explains something. You may choose to write a recipe, directions for making a paper airplane, or describe an experiment and its results.

A *persuasive writing* gives an opinion and tries to get others to agree with it. Facts and examples are given to support the opinion. A model for this may be a letter to the editor, a letter to my parents (or children) making a request, or a book or movie review.

Choose one kind of writing to model for students. For example, write a description of a favorite member of your family. As you write, think out loud about what you need to tell the reader so she knows about and can "see" your family member. Model how to think about capitalization, punctuation, and spelling. Model how to use the word wall as a spelling resource. Circle any words you think you did not spell correctly.

Your modeling should not take more than five minutes. If you are unable to complete your writing in five minutes continue to work on it in the next session(s).

Additional information on different styles of writing may be found in *Teaching Writing: Balancing Process and Product* (Tompkins, 1999).

Paragraph Writing

Materials: chalkboard or chart paper

One of the skills older children will be expected to learn is how to create a paragraph. To teach students how to write a complete paragraph you are going to model how to write one for them.

Tell students you are going to write a paragraph while they watch. Explain to students that a paragraph is like a sandwich cookie. It has a topic sentence (the outside cookie), a body of information (the creamy filling), and a closing sentence (the other cookie). (This is a good time to snack while you model.)

The topic sentence tells the reader what the paragraph is going to be about. The body gives the reader all of the information they need to understand the topic. The closing sentence summarizes the information in the paragraph.

Write a paragraph for students modeling the three parts. The paragraph you write may be descriptive (describes a person, place, thing, or idea), narrative (tells a story), persuasive (gives and opinion about something), or expository (gives directions, tells how to do something, or explains something).

Note: Don't make children learn the labels for the different kinds of paragraphs unless they will be held accountable for them.

Modeling paragraph writing allows children to see how a writer puts her thoughts together into written form. Be sure to identify the topic sentence, body, and closing sentence of your paragraph. You will also want to model what to do when you don't know how to spell a word. First, see if it is a word on the Word Wall. If not, model how to stretch out the word and then circle it because you aren't sure. The circle means you will look that word up later. Model how to check to make sure each sentence is on the topic. Identify the topic and read the paragraph sentence-by-sentence checking to see if it matches the topic.

Your modeling should not take more than five minutes. If you are unable to complete your writing in five minutes continue to work on it in the next session(s).

Writing with Children

Predictable Charts

A predictable chart, like a predictable book, uses the same words over and over so children become familiar with them and are successful in reading them. For ideas and information on predictable charts see *Predictable Charts: Shared Writing for Kindergarten and First Grade* by Dorothy Hall and Elaine Williams (2000).

Materials: chart paper

1. Choose a beginning for each sentence on the chart. Read the beginning words and finish the first sentence yourself. Write your name in parentheses at the end of the sentence. Now write sentences for each child. Write the author's name after each sentence.

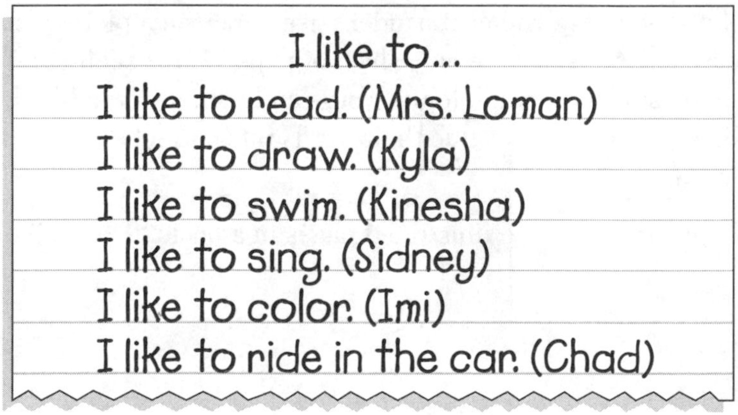
I like to...
I like to read. (Mrs. Loman)
I like to draw. (Kyla)
I like to swim. (Kinesha)
I like to sing. (Sidney)
I like to color. (Imi)
I like to ride in the car. (Chad)

Suggested beginnings for Predictable Charts:

I like…	We saw…
I can…	Friends…
I want…	Brothers…
I eat…	Sisters…
I play…	Mothers…
I would…	Fathers…
I have…	My teacher…

Some beginnings will come from the stories you read during Guided Reading:

Nora…

Clifford…

Ducks like…

Snow…

2. Practice reading the sentences. Have the "author" read his sentence to the class. Have him point to the words as he reads. Then, have the class read it with him.

   Note: If students have trouble pointing to the words as they read place a small dot under each word. Have them touch the dot as they read.

3. After reading all of the sentences write each student's sentence on a piece of paper (sentence strip) or have each student write his own sentence on a sheet of paper. Have each child cut his sentence into separate words. Have the students scramble the words and then unscramble them to recreate their sentences. If time allows, have students glue their words into correct sentences on pieces of paper and illustrate their sentences.

4. Make group books by placing all of the illustrated pages in a book. "Donate" the book to the class for their library.

Daily Summaries

Materials: chalkboard or chart paper

Write a daily summary with children. Tell them what you are going to summarize today:

- class activities
- the story read
- current events

Ask students to tell you what they remember about the event or story. Take student ideas and put them into written form. Talk out loud while you are writing their ideas. Continue to model how to think about what you are writing (content) and how you are writing it (capitals, punctuation, and spelling).

Your writing should not take more than five minutes. Limit your summary to two or three sentences.

Paragraph Writing

Materials: chalkboard or chart paper

As children develop their writing skills they will be ready to learn how to create a paragraph. Use students' ideas to show them how to organize their thoughts into a paragraph.

Ask children to give you four or five sentences about any topic.

"Dogs have tails."

"Dogs have fur."

"Dogs are animals."

"Some dogs are big. Some dogs are small."

Discuss the sentences with students. Explain to them that all of the sentences are about dogs so the first sentence should tell them that.

Dogs are animals.

The next sentences should describe dogs. Because we already know that the sentences are about dogs we don't have to keep writing the word *dog*.

Dogs are animals. They have tails. They have fur.

The last two sentences can be combined to be one good sentence.

Dogs are animals. They have tails. They have fur. Some dogs are big and some are small.

Finally, we should add a sentence to tell the reader that we are finished talking about dogs.

Dogs are animals. They have tails. They have fur. Some dogs are big and some are small. Dogs are very special animals."

Over the next several days or over the course of the next few weeks, model several different paragraphs. This will allow students to see different examples on several different topics.

Your modeling should not take more than five minutes. If you are unable to complete your writing in five minutes, continue to work on it in the next session(s).

More Paragraph Writing

Materials: chalkboard or chart paper

Tell children you are going to write a paragraph together. Students may make suggestions for what you are to write or you may choose to write:

narrative paragraph: summary of a story read in Guided Reading

descriptive paragraph: show students a picture and have them describe it for someone else

expository paragraph: write directions for making a peanut butter and jelly sandwich

persuasive paragraph: write a letter to the cafeteria requesting a new food item

Remind them that a good paragraph has a topic sentence, a body, and a closing sentence. As you write the paragraph identify what you are writing.

Writing with children allows you to guide the process with student input. As a review have them identify a topic sentence, the body, and a closing sentence of the paragraph. Check to make sure that each sentence is on the topic.

The writing section of your time with students should not take more than five minutes. If you are unable to complete the writing in five minutes, continue to work on it in the next session(s).

Writing by Children

Written Conversation

Materials: individual student journals

Begin a written conversation with a student by asking her a question in her journal. Ask her to answer the question and ask you one in return. Write to each student every two to three sessions to keep the dialogue going back and forth.

Journal Writing

Materials: individual student journals

Ask students to write something they want to tell in their journal. Explain to them that if you can say it you can write it.

Before beginning journal writing take some time to make a class list of all of the things students can write about. The list might include:

- What I did last night
- My day at school
- My favorite thing to do after school
- My favorite thing to do at school
- My pet
- My best friend
- My family
- My favorite thing to eat
- My favorite movie
- My favorite book

Remind students to use the Word Wall to spell any words they aren't sure about. If the word isn't on the wall they are to "guess" the spelling using what they know about letters and sounds. Have them circle any words that they aren't sure about.

Be sure to leave time at the end of the session for each student to read what she wrote.

Take time to write to each student in his journal sometime during the week. You may want to respond to something he told you in his writing. This is a good way to encourage students to tell you more.

Paragraph Writing

Materials: writing paper

Have children think of a topic they would like to write about. Have them write four sentences about the topic. They may write these in their journal or on a sheet of paper.

Review with students how you put their sentences together to write a paragraph. Tell them it is their turn to make a paragraph. Encourage children to think about how the ideas in the sentences are connected as they choose how to organize their thoughts to write their paragraph.

More Paragraph Writing

Materials: writing paper

Ask children to brainstorm ideas for writing their own paragraph. They can tell a story (narrative); describe a person, place, thing, or idea (descriptive); give directions, tell how to do something, or explain something (expository); or give an opinion about something (persuasive).

Once children have decided upon a topic, ask them to write the opening sentence. Then have them think of at least two or three more sentences that provide additional information about the topic. Finally, ask them to write a closing sentence.

Allow time at the end of each session to have students read what they have written. Have other students ask them questions that would make their writing clearer and more enjoyable to read.

Why do you like skiing?

When did you go Disneyland®?

What does your little sister look like?

When the paragraphs are complete, find an "audience" to read them to.

Teacher Resources

Rhyming Picture Cards

Top row: sheep, bee, hat, coat   Middle row: goat, can, light, fan   Bottom row: jeep, key, bat, kite

Words for Counting Syllables

One-Syllable Words

ant	chair	friend	mom
bed	dad	girl	mouse
big	day	glass	paint
boy	dog	hand	play
brush	door	he	shark
can	ear	ice	she
car	fan	key	tape
cat	foot	light	vase

Two-Syllable Words

airplane	city	little	pretty
baby	cookie	mirror	sister
baseball	dentist	outside	sometimes
because	doctor	paper	table
birthday	flashlight	pencil	taco
brother	flower	people	very
basket	gerbil	picture	teacher
children	grandma	pizza	window

Three-Syllable Words

alphabet	computer	hairdresser	photograph
animal	decompose	interstate	probably
anyone	discover	invasion	radio
basketball	elephant	kangaroo	recycle
beautiful	entertain	karate	restaurant
bicycle	exciting	lovable	substitute
celery	favorite	microphone	telephone
chemical	governor	origin	vacation

Two-Sound Picture Cards

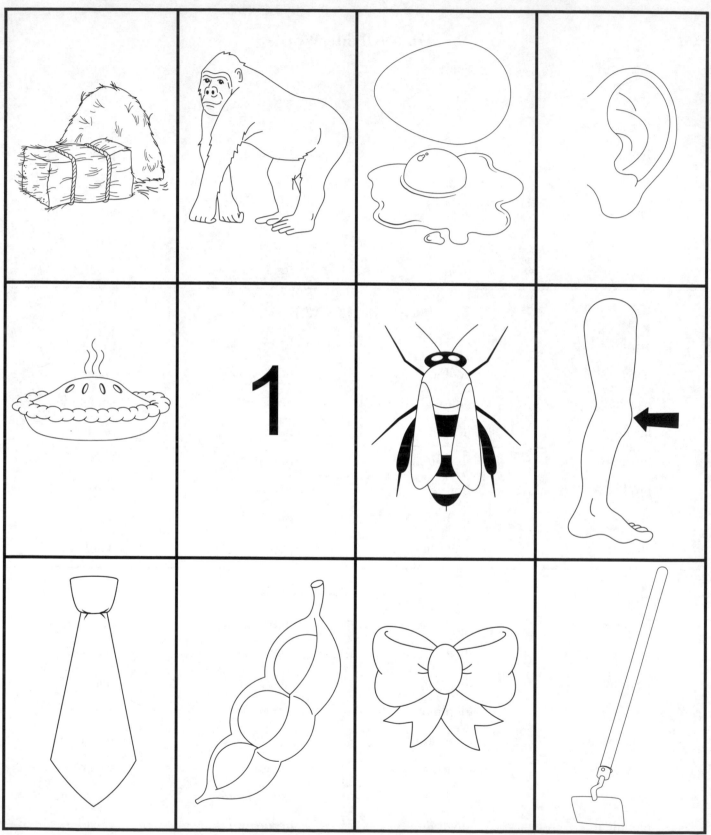

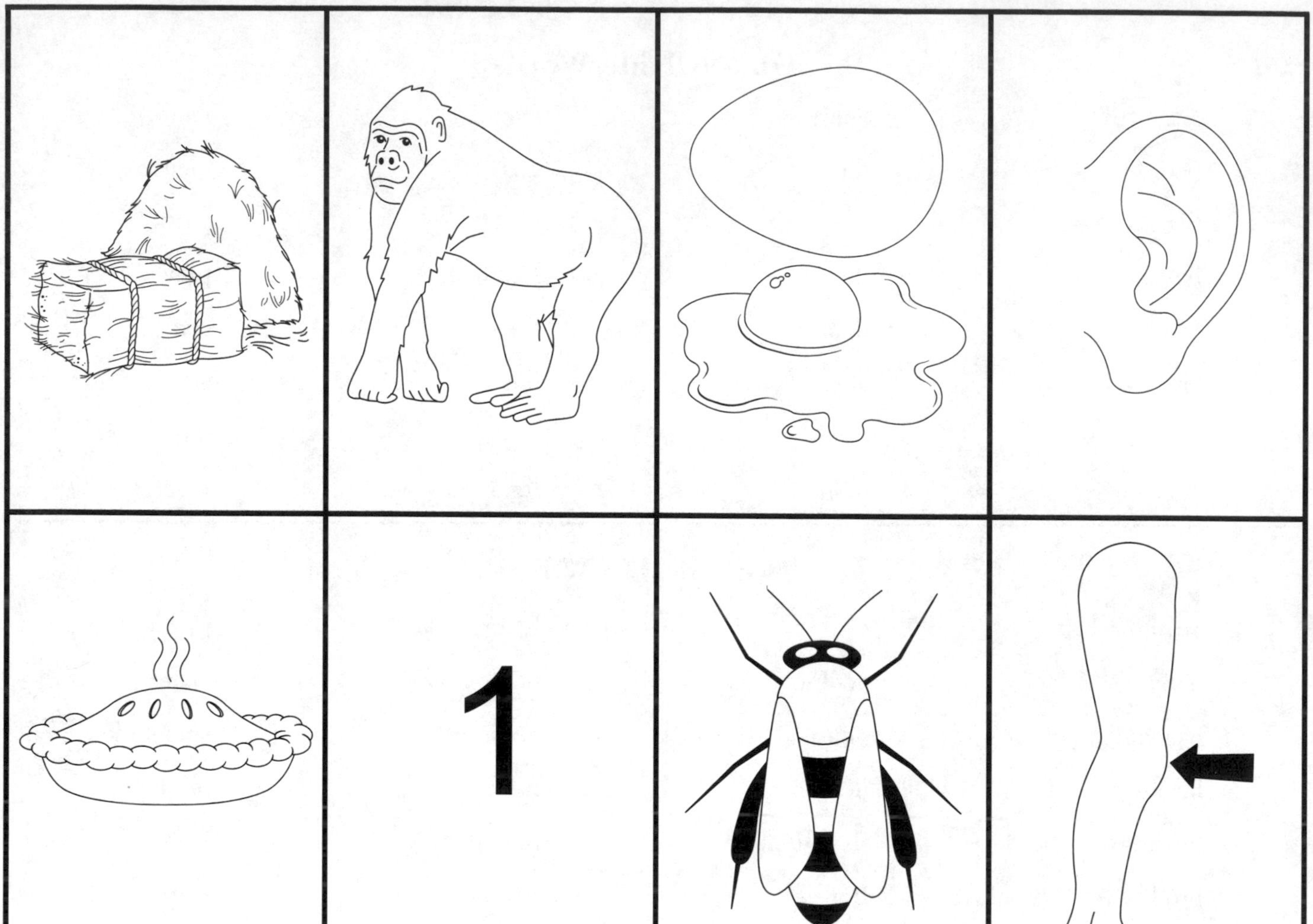

Top row: hay, ape, egg, ear Middle row: pie, one, bee, knee Bottom row: tie, pea, bow, hoe

Three-Sound Picture Cards

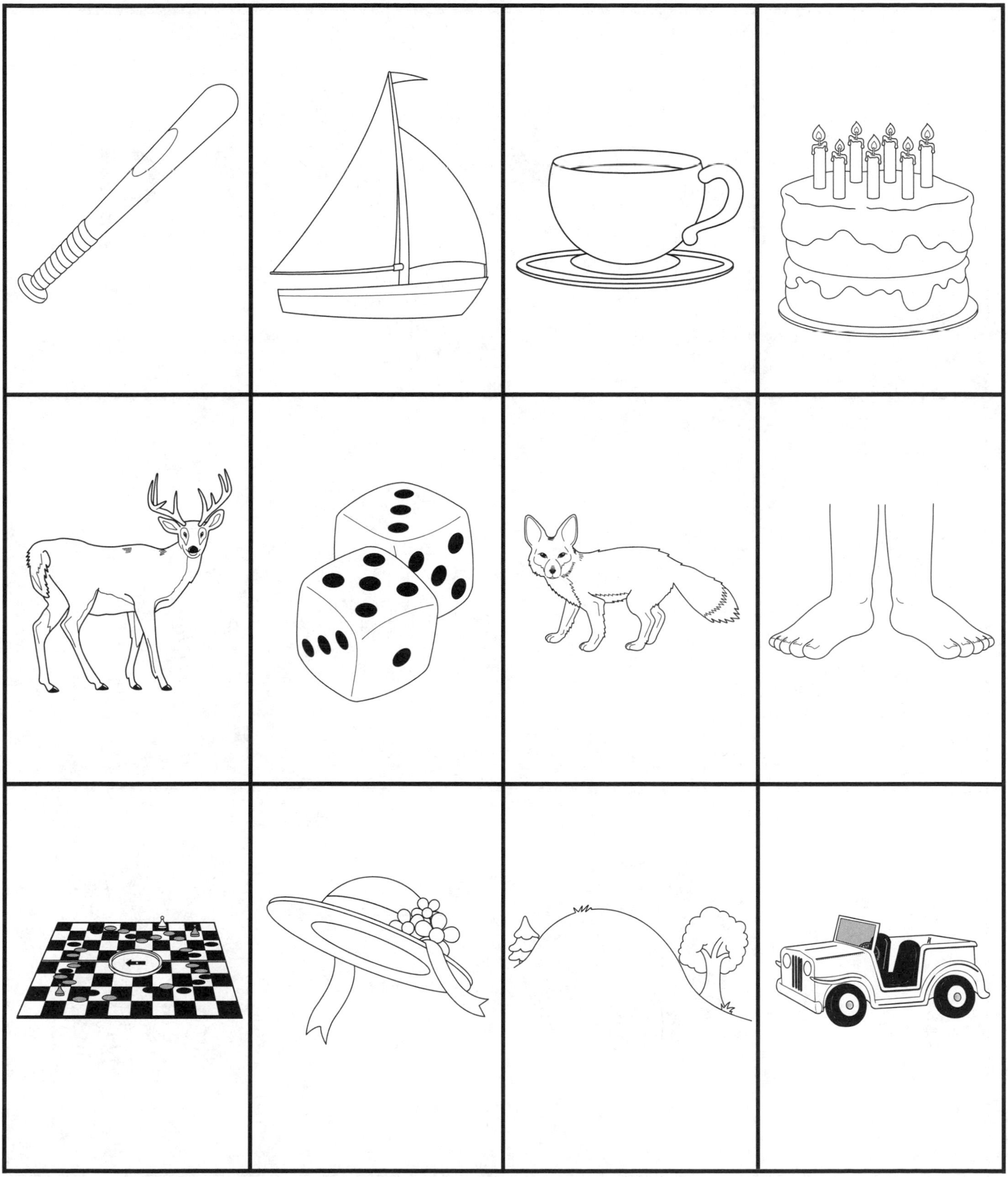

Top row: bat, boat, cup, cake   Middle row: deer, dice, fox, feet   Bottom row: game, hat, hill, jeep

Three-Sound Picture Cards

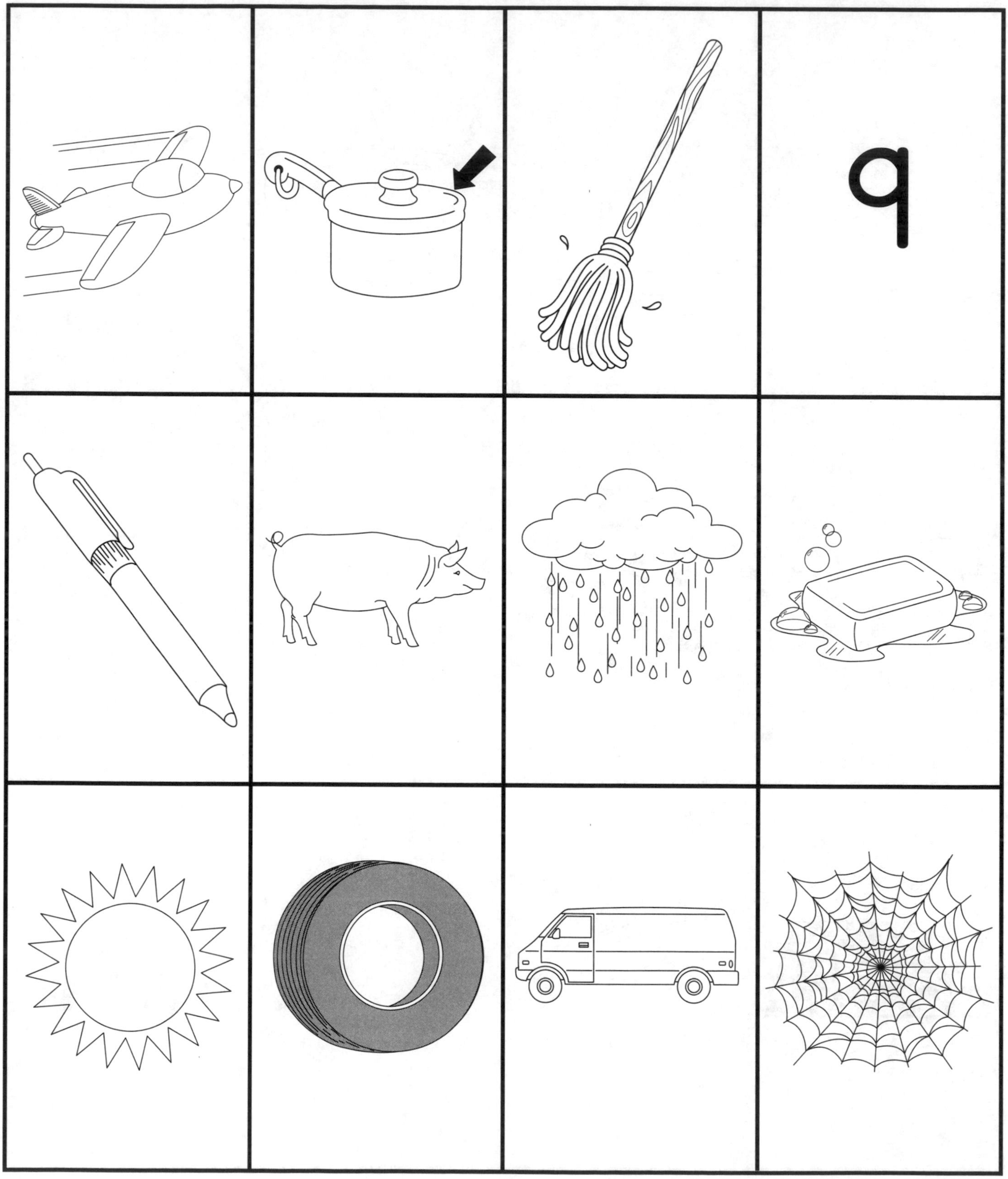

Top row: jet, lid, mop, nine   Middle row: pen, pig, rain, soap   Bottom row: sun, tire, van, web

Words for Adding Sounds to Make New Words

Add the following sounds to the words shown to make new words. (e.g., *all* with a /b/ in front makes *ball*). Delete the beginning sounds from the new words to leave the initial words (e.g., *ball* minus /b/ makes *all*).

Word	Sounds for Adding											
ad	/b/	/d/	/f/	/h/	/l/	/m/	/p/	/s/				
all	/b/	/c/	/f/	/h/	/m/	/t/	/w/					
and	/b/	/h/	/l/	/s/								
ark	/b/	/d/	/l/	/m/	/p/							
ash	/b/	/c/	/d/	/fl/	/g/	/m/	/r/	/s/	/st/	/tr/		
at	/b/	/c/	/f/	/h/	/m/	/p/	/r/	/s/	/v/			
ill	/b/	/d/	/f/	/g/	/h/	/J/	/k/	/m/	/p/	/s/	/t/	/w/
in	/b/	/ch/	/f/	/gr/	/k/	/p/	/sk/	/t/	/w/			
it	/b/	/f/	/h/	/k/	/p/	/s/	/sp/					
oat	/b/	/c/	/fl/									
ox	/b/	/f/										
other	/br/	/m/	/sm/									
able	/c/	/f/	/t/									
an	/c/	/f/	/m/	/p/	/r/	/St/	/t/	/v/				
air	/ch/	/f/	/h/	/p/	/st/							
arm	/ch/	/f/	/h/									
up	/c/	/p/										
ear	/d/	/f/	/h/	/n/	/r/							
ice	/d/	/m/	/n/	/r/	/sl/	/sp/	/tw/					
act	/f/	/p/	/t/									
ate	/f/	/g/	/gr/	/h/	/l/	/pl/	/r/	/sk/				
eel	/f/	/h/	/p/	/st/	/wh/							
inch	/f/	/p/										
or	/f/											
use	/f/											
edge	/h/	/l/	/pl/	/w/								
ink	/p/	/r/	/s/	/st/	/w/							

Words to Substitute Sounds

pig	If you take away the /p/and add /b/ you make *big.*
big	If you take away the /b/and add /w/ you make *wig.*
wig	If you take away the /w/and add /d/ you make *dig.*
bed	If you take away the /b/and add /r/ you make *red.*
red	If you take away the /r/and add /f/ you make *fed.*
fed	If you take away the /f/and add /l/ you make *led.*
dice	If you take away the /d/and add /r/ you make *rice.*
rice	If you take away the /r/and add /m/ you make *mice.*
mice	If you take away the /m/and add /n/ you make *nice.*
dog	If you take away the /d/and add /l/ you make *log.*
log	If you take away the /l/and add /h/ you make *hog.*
hog	If you take away the /h/and add /j/ you make *jog.*
art	If you add /d/ you make *dart.*
dart	If you take away the /d/and add /p/ you make *part.*
part	If you take away the /p/and add /c/ you make *cart.*
hop	If you take away the /h/and add /t/ you make *top.*
top	If you take away the /t/and add /p/ you make *pop.*
pop	If you take away the /p/and add /st/ you make *stop.*
root	If you take away the /r/and add /sh/ you make *shoot.*
shoot	If you take away the /sh/and add /sc/ you make *scoot.*
scoot	If you take away the /sc/and add /h/ you make *hoot.*
ducks	If you take away the /d/and add /b/ you make *bucks.*
bucks	If you take away the /b/and add /pl/ you make *plucks.*
plucks	If you take away the /pl/and add /tr/ you make *trucks.*
weed	If you take away the /w/and add /f/ you make *feed.*
feed	If you take away the /f/and add /s/ you make *seed.*
seed	If you take away the /s/and add /n/ you make *need.*
battle	If you take away the /b/and add /r/ you make *rattle.*
rattle	If you take away the /r/and add /t/ you make *tattle.*
tattle	If you take away the /t/and add /c/ you make *cattle.*

Tic-Tac-Toe Cards

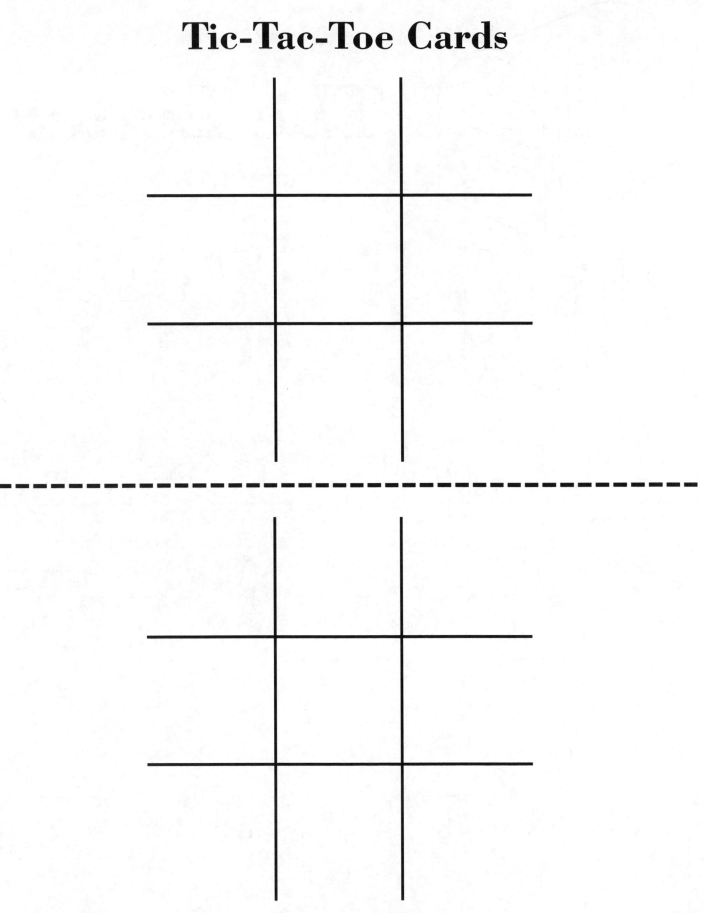

The Letter

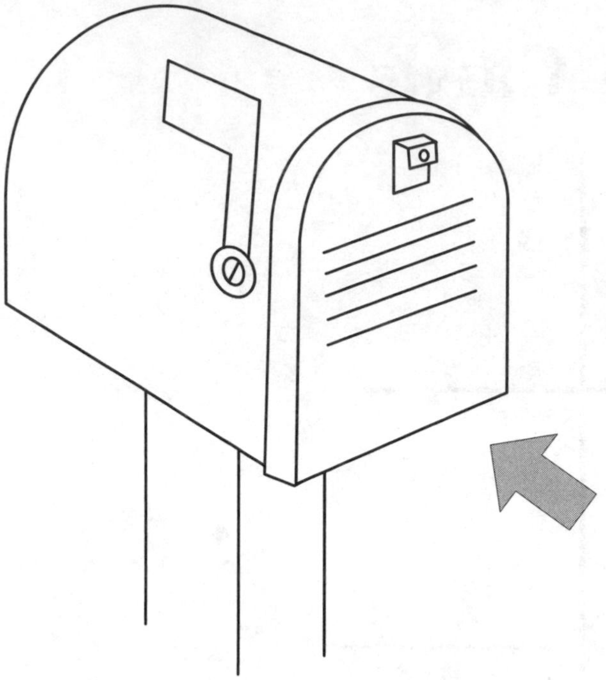

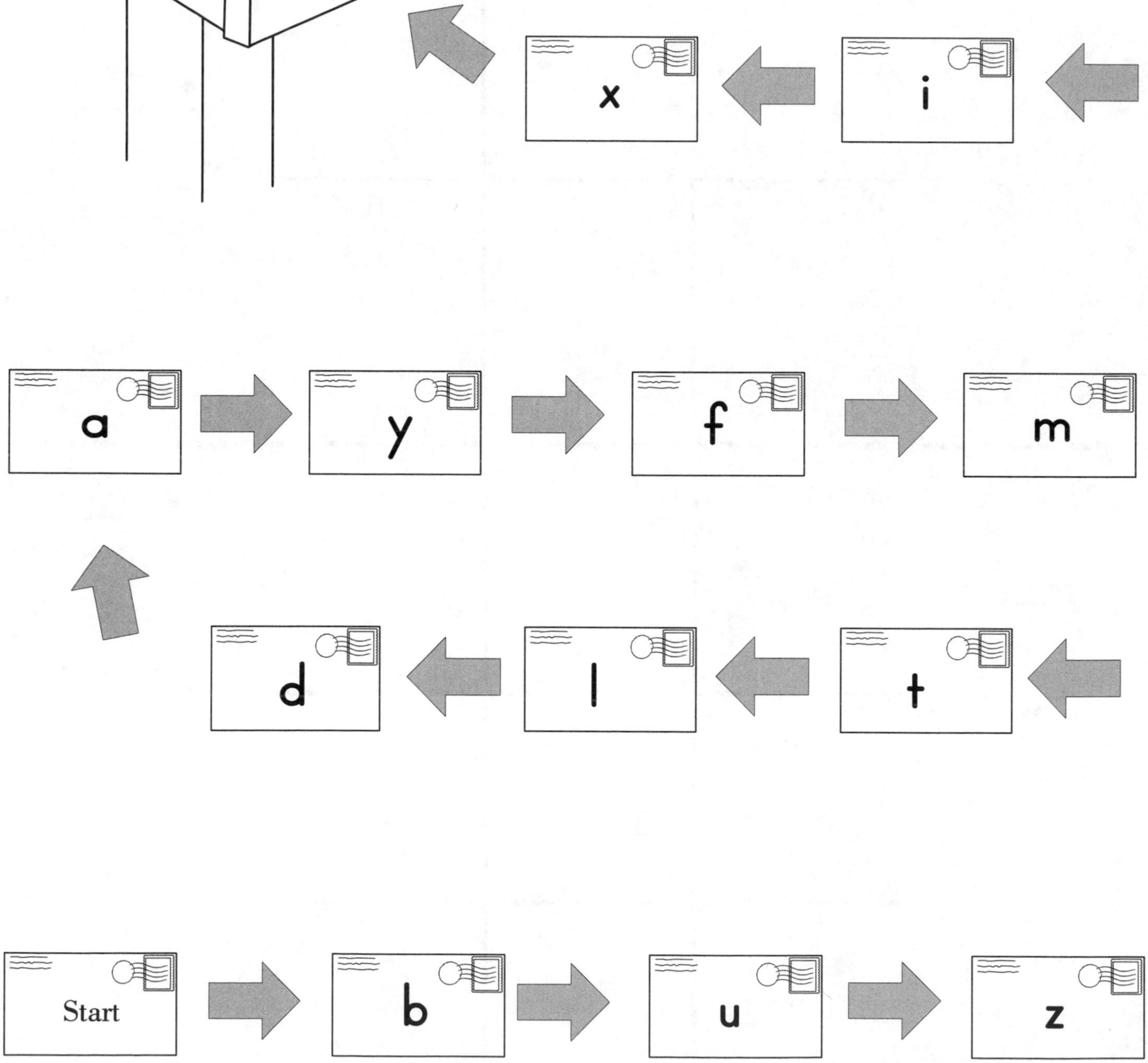

Game

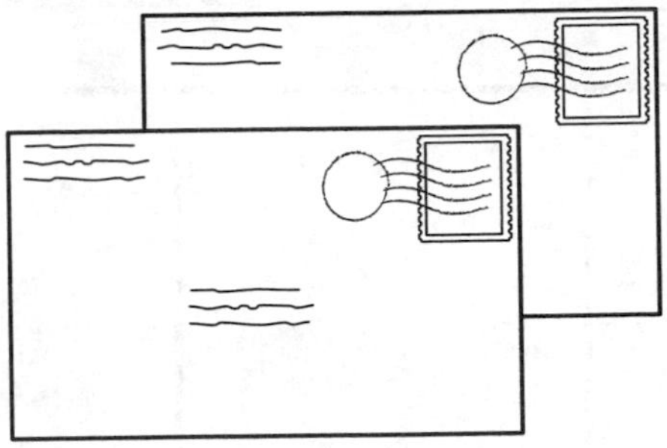

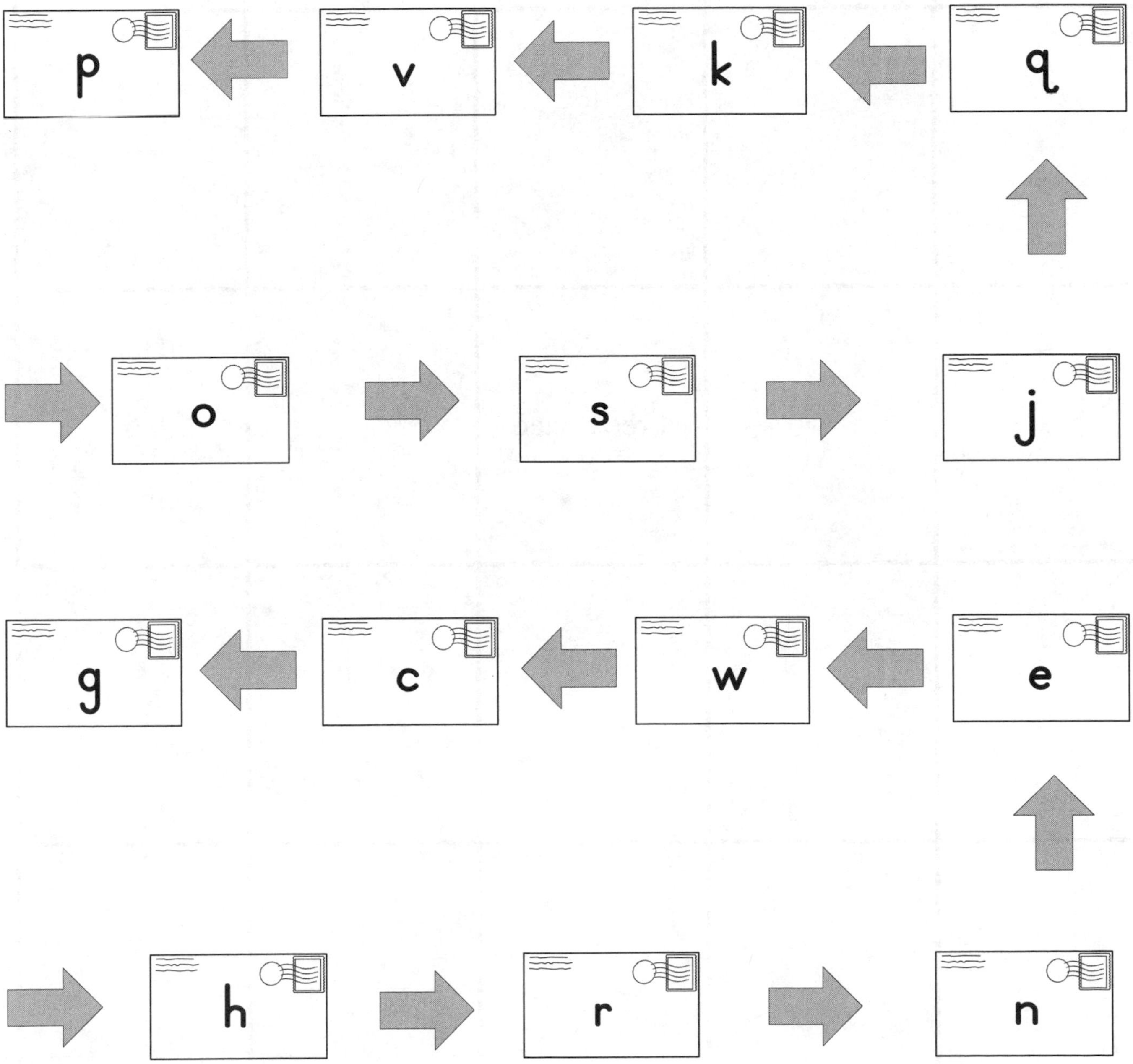

Bingo Card

		Free Space		

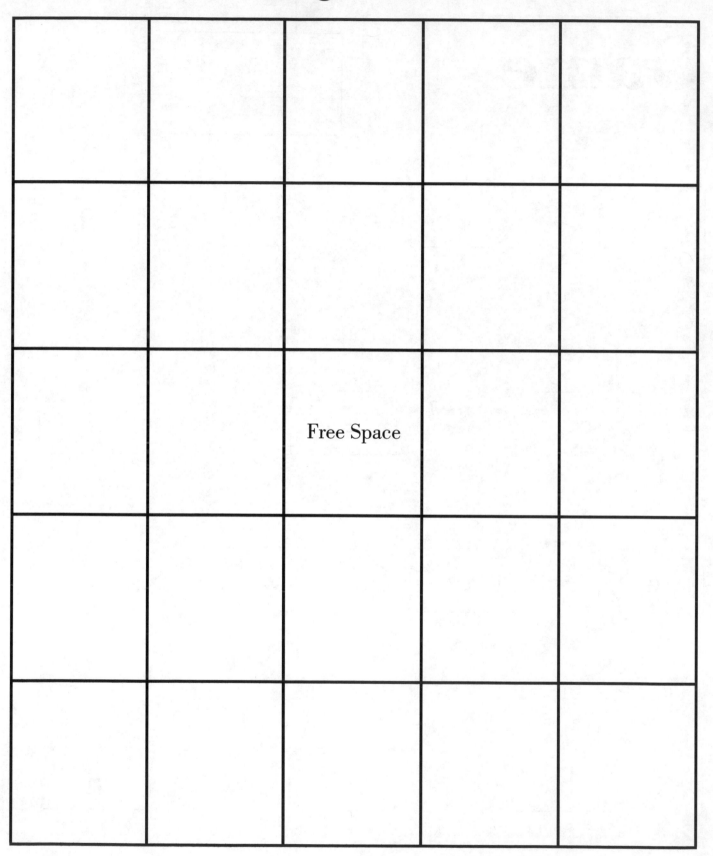

Beginning Letter Sounds Picture Cards

Consonants

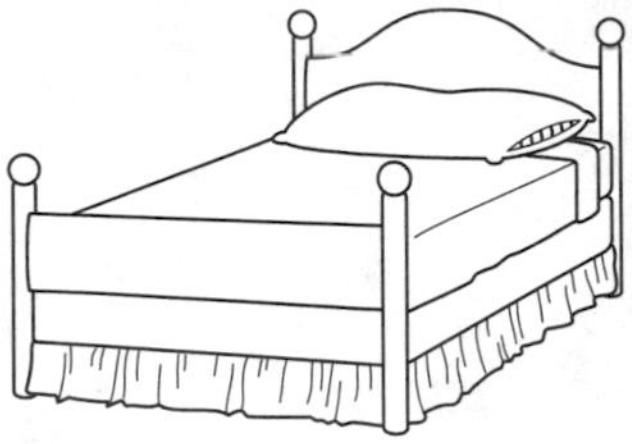

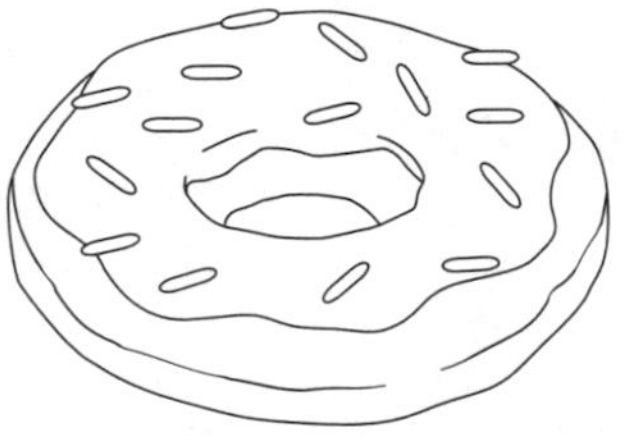

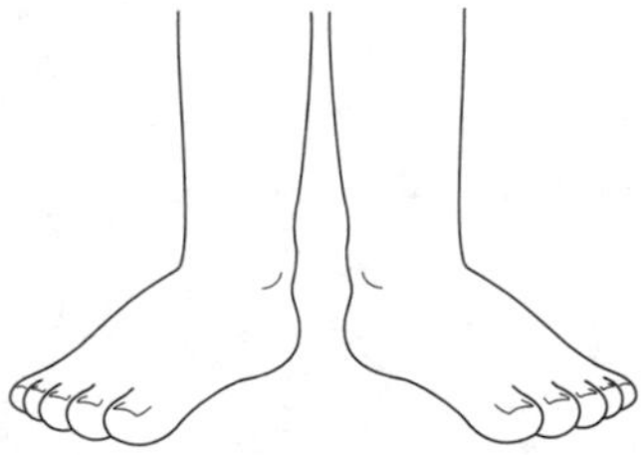

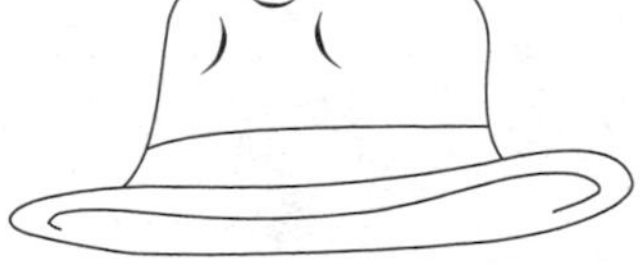

Top row: banana, bed, camera, cake   Middle row: dog, doughnut, fish, feet   Bottom row: goat, game, house, hat

Beginning Letter Sounds Picture Cards

Consonants

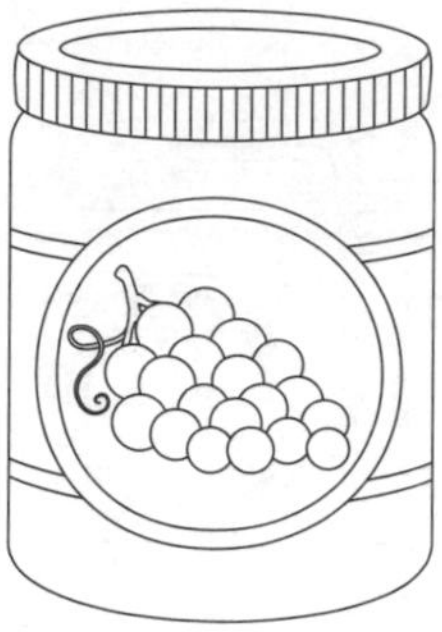

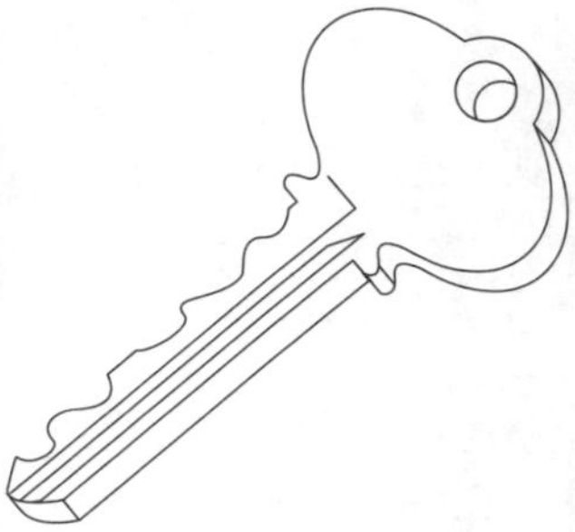

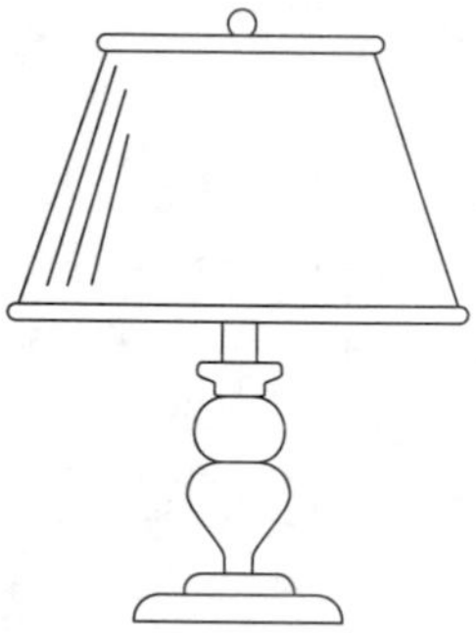

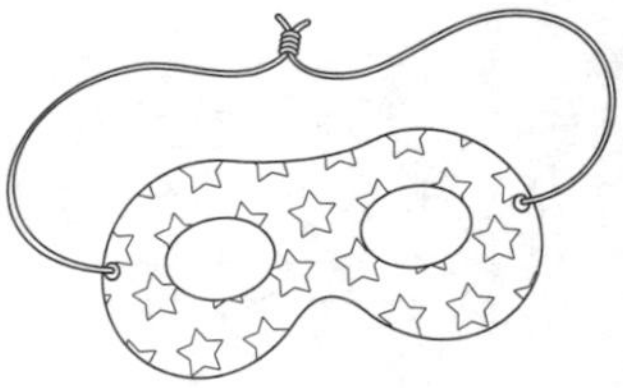

9

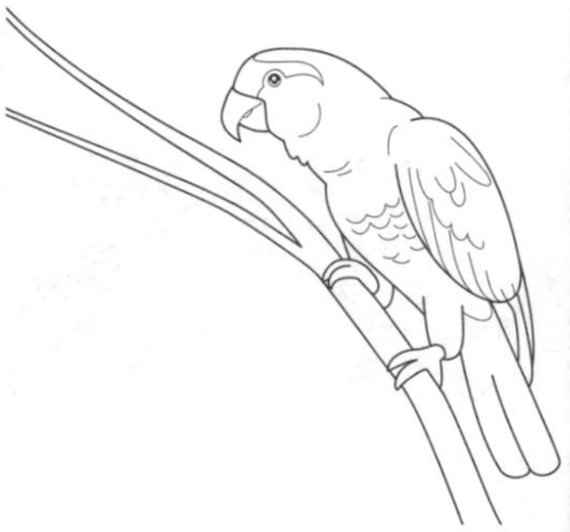

Top row: jeep, jar, kangaroo, key Middle row: lamp, lion, mouse, mask Bottom row: newspaper, nine, parrot, pencil

Beginning Letter Sounds Picture Cards

Consonants

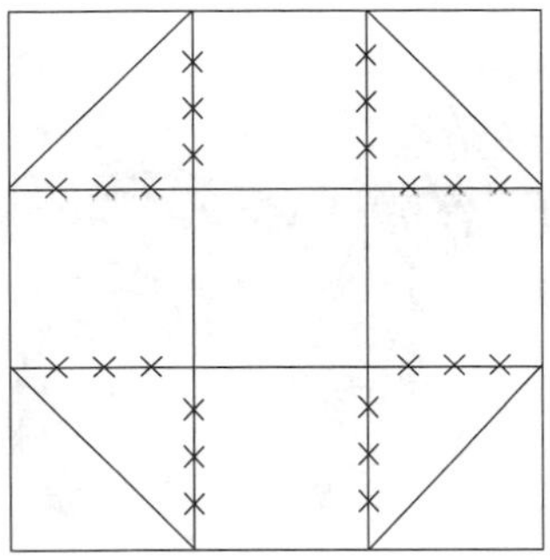
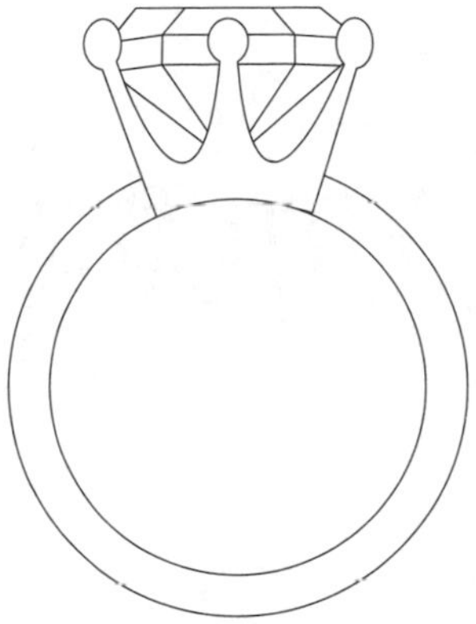

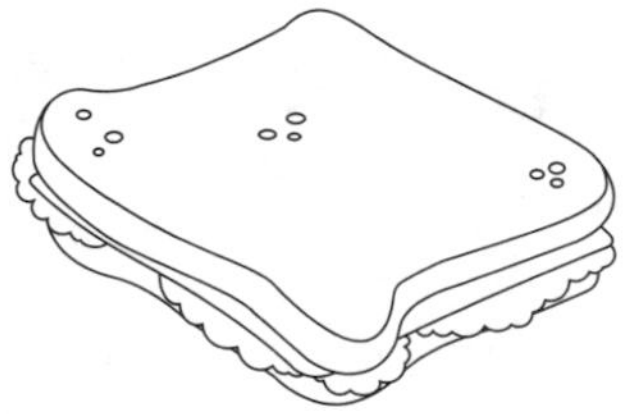

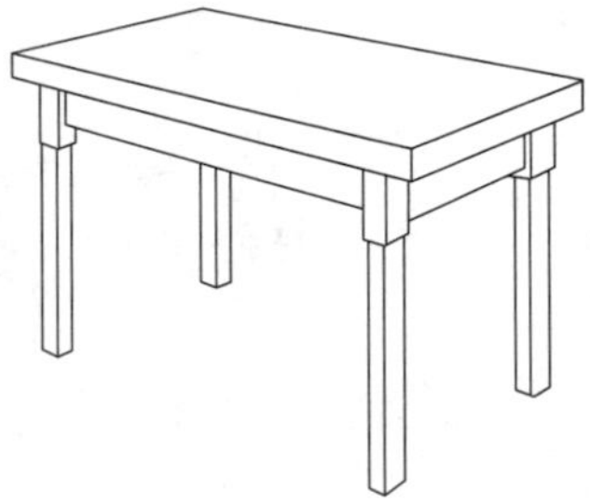

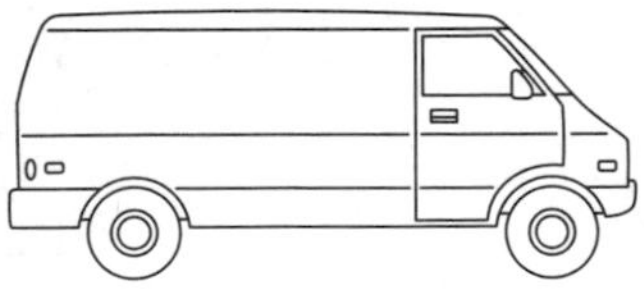

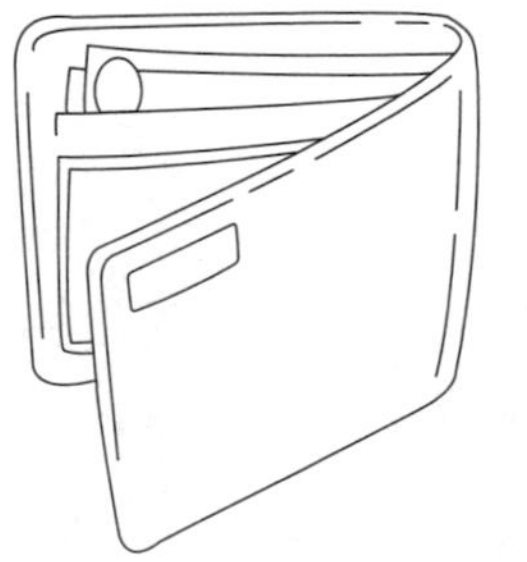

Top row: queen, quilt, ring, rooster   Middle row: sun, sandwich, tiger, table   Bottom row: van, vulture, window, wallet

Beginning Letter Sounds Picture Cards

Consonants

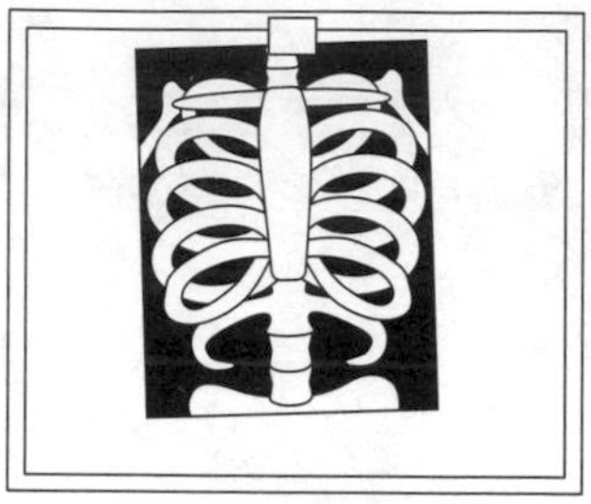
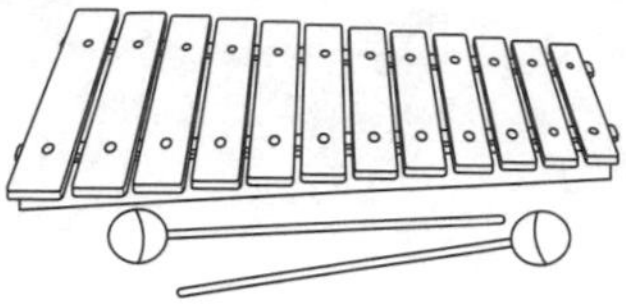

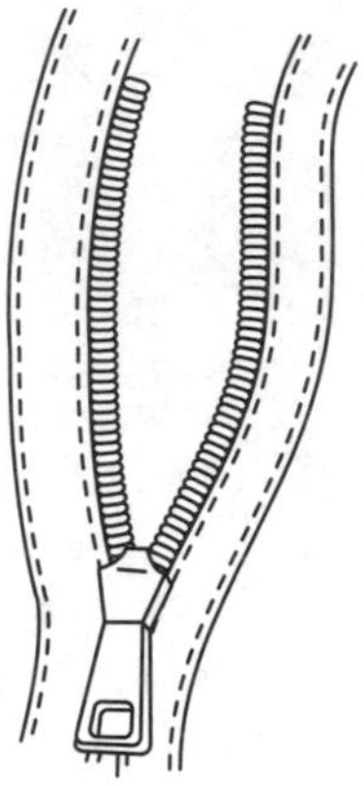

Vowels

Top row: x-ray, xylophone, zebra, zipper   Middle row: apple, ant, ape, acorn   Bottom row: elephant, egg, eagle, ear

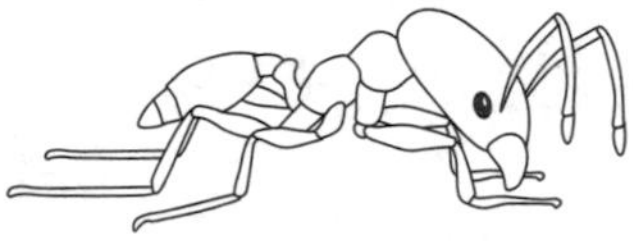

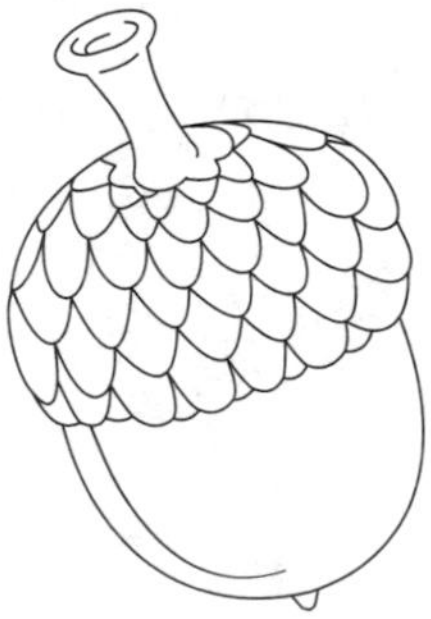

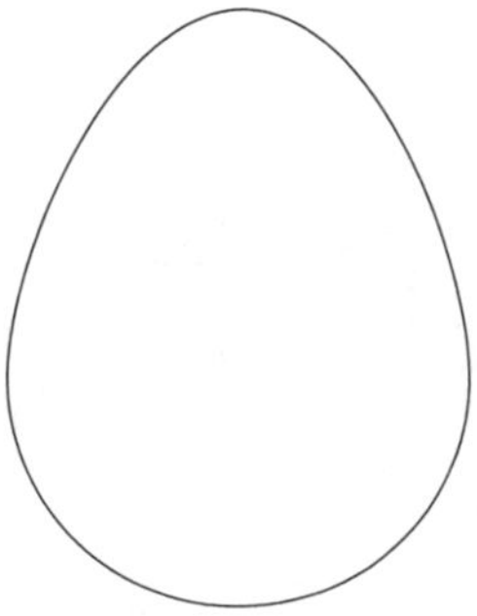

Beginning Letter Sounds Picture Cards

Vowels

Top row: igloo, insect, ice cream, ice   Middle row: octopus, ostrich, oval, orange   Bottom row: United States, underwear, unicorn, umbrella

The Word Bird Game

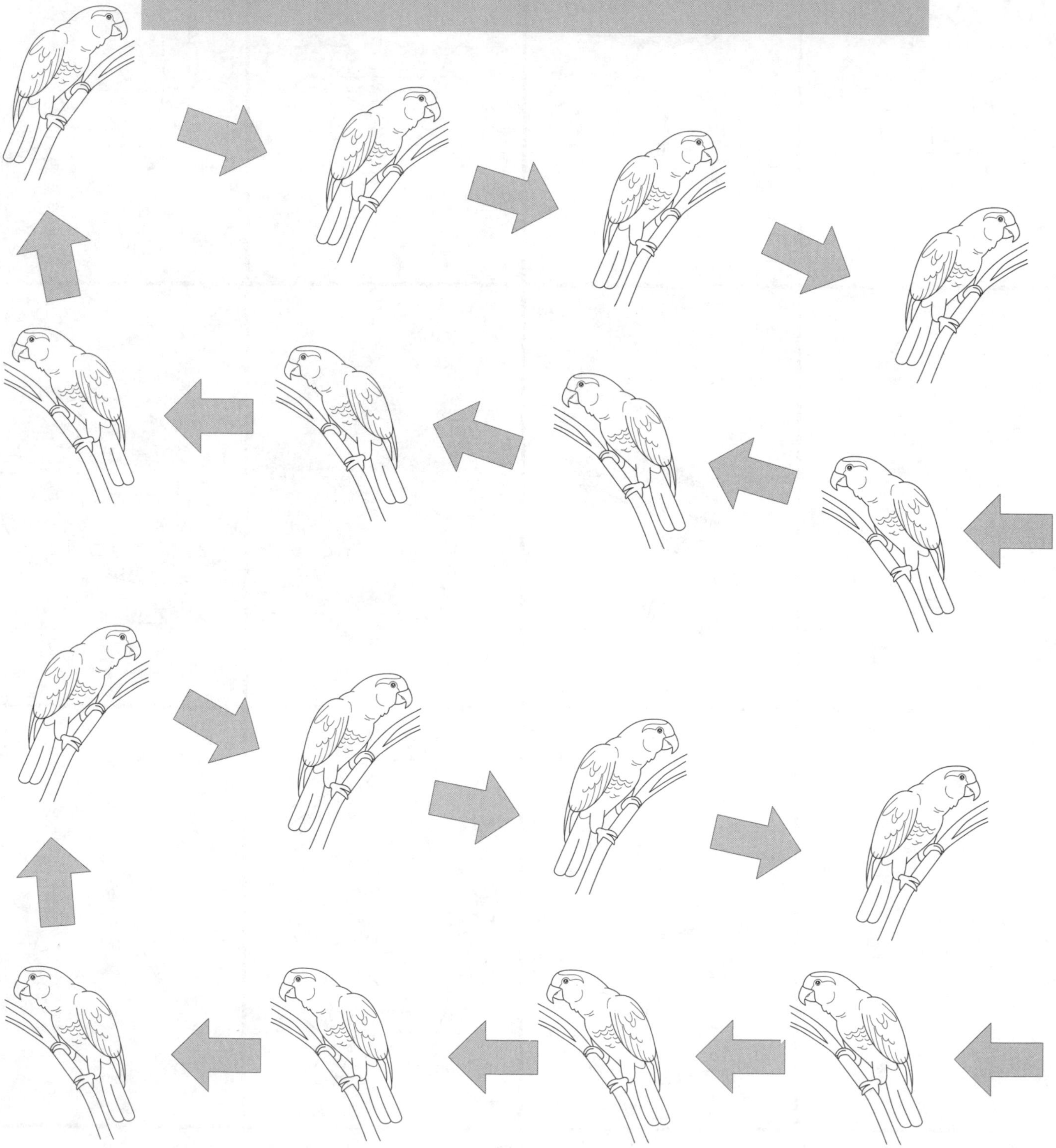

Word Cards

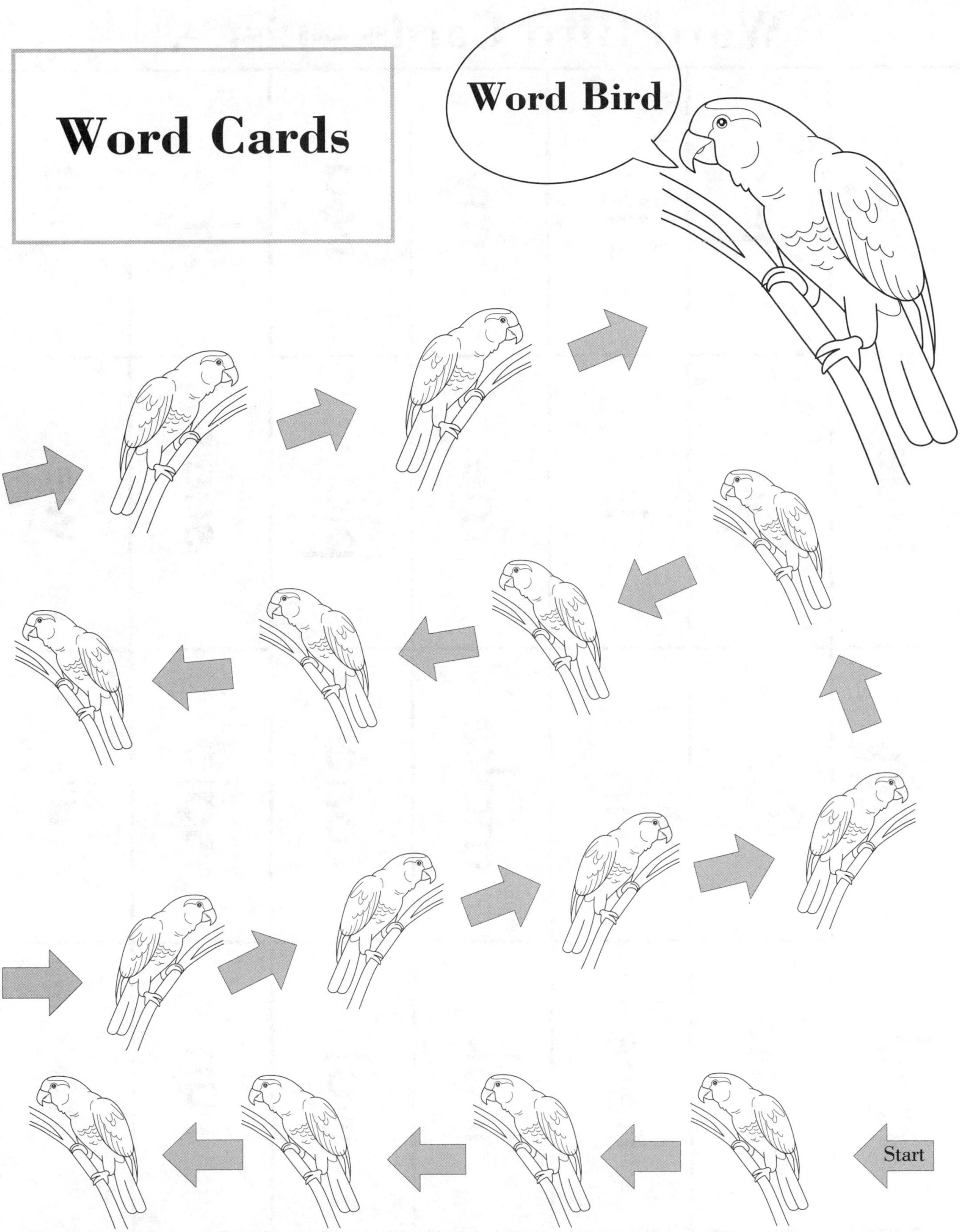

Word Bird Cards—List A

can	help	it	my	red	the	you
blue	go	is	me	play	see	we
big	for	in	make	one	said	up
and	come	here	look	not	run	to

Word Bird Cards—List B

at	did	good	like	our	say	that
are	came	get	into	on	saw	soon
am	but	eat	he	no	ran	so
all	be	do	have	new	please	she

Word Bird Cards—List B (continued)

want		
this	will	
they	well	
there	was	

Word Bird Cards—List C

as	could	had	how	live	old	put
any	by	give	him	let	of	over
an	blue	from	her	know	must	open
again	ask	every	has	just	may	once

Word Bird Cards—List C (continued)

thank	walk	had
take	think	with
stop	then	when
some	them	were

The Letter Game and Word Bird Dice

Cut on solid lines and fold on dotted lines.

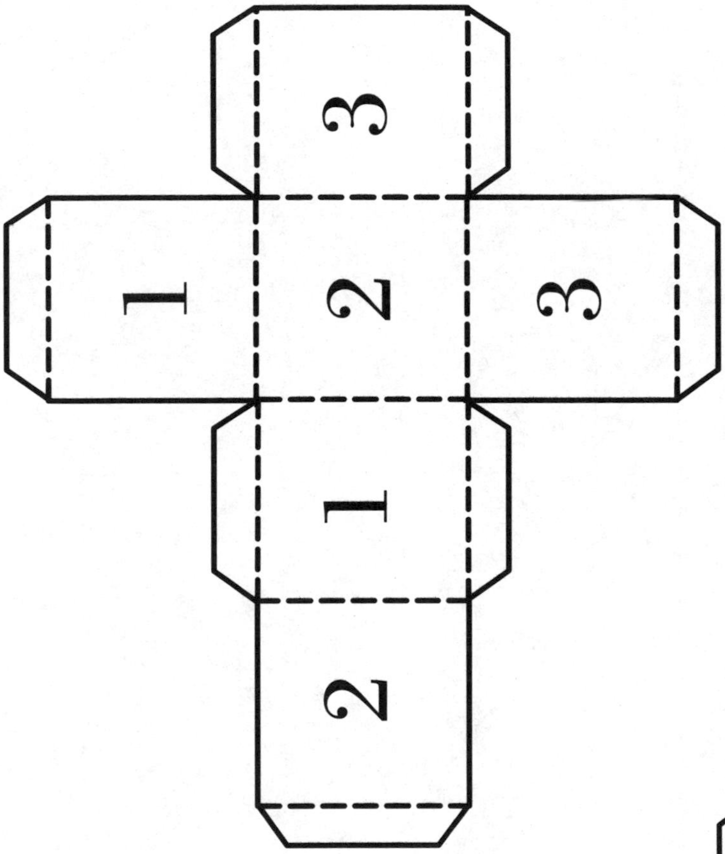

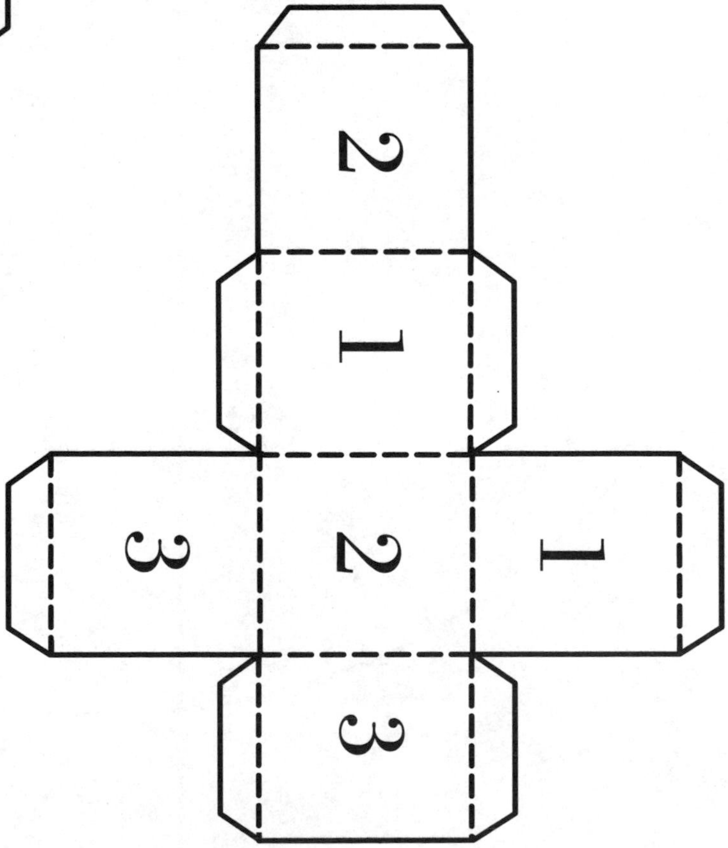

Word Wheel

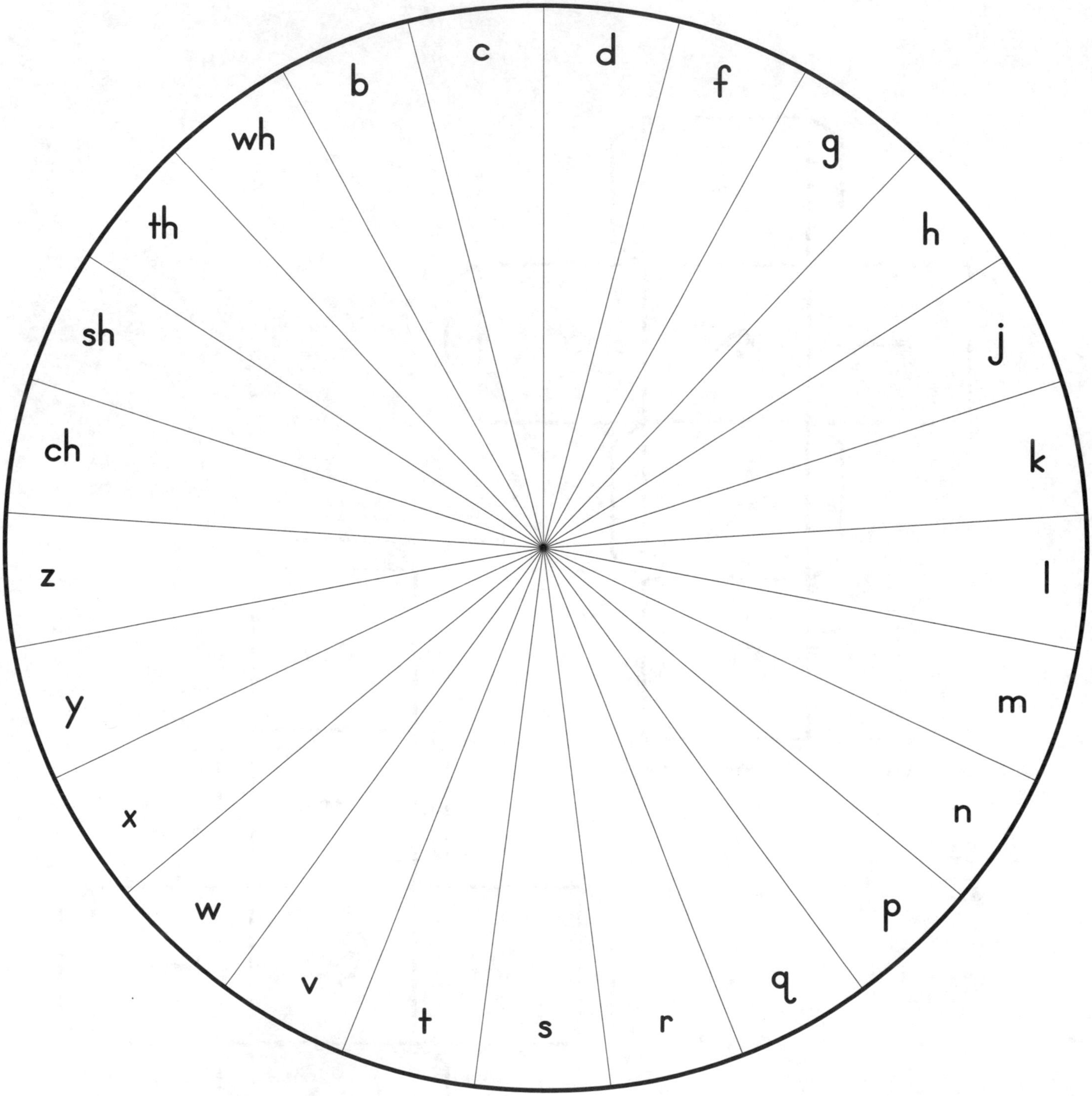

Professional References

Adams, M. J. (1990). *Beginning to Read: Thinking and Learning about Print*. Cambridge, MA: MIT Press.

Beaver, J. (1997). *Developmental Reading Assessment*. New Jersey: Celebration Press.

Clay, M. M.(1985). *The Early Detection of Reading Difficulties (3rd ed.)*. Portsmouth, NH: Heinemann.

Clay, M. M. (1993). *An Observation Survey: Of Early Literacy Achievement*. Portsmouth, NH: Heinemann.

Cunningham, P. M. (2000). *Phonics They Use: Words for Reading and Writing (3rd ed.)* New York, NY: Longman.

Cunningham, P. M. (2000). *Systematic Sequential Phonics They Use: For Beginning Readers of All Ages*. Greensboro, NC: Carson-Dellosa Publishing.

Cunningham, P. M. & Hall, D. P. (1994). *Making Words*. Torrance, CA: Good Apple.

Cunningham, P. M. & Hall, D. P. (1997). *Making More Words*. Torrance, CA: Good Apple.

Cunningham, P. M. & Hall, D. P. (1998). *Month-by-Month Phonics for First Grade*. Greensboro, NC: Carson-Dellosa Publishing.

Cunningham, P. M. & Hall, D. P. (1998). *Month-by-Month Phonics for Second Grade*. Greensboro, NC: Carson-Dellosa Publishing.

Cunningham, P. M. & Hall, D. P. (1998). *Month-by-Month Phonics for Third Grade*. Greensboro, NC: Carson-Dellosa Publishing.

Cunningham, P. M. & Hall, D. P. (1998). *Month-by-Month Phonics for Upper Grades*. Greensboro, NC: Carson-Dellosa Publishing.

Cunningham, P. M. & Hall, D. P. (1997). *Month-by-Month Reading and Writing for Kindergarten*. Greensboro, NC: Carson-Dellosa Publishing.

Cunningham, P. M., Hall, D. P. & Sigmon, C. M. (1999). *The Teachers Guide to the Four Blocks*. Greensboro, NC: Carson-Dellosa Publishing.

Hall, D. P. & Williams, E. (2001). *Predictable Charts: Shared Writing for Kindergarten and First Grade*. Greensboro, NC: Carson-Dellosa Publishing.

Hoffman, J., Cunningham, P. M., Cunningham, J. W., & Yopp, H. (1998). *Phonemic Awareness and the Teaching of Reading*. Newark, DE: International Reading Association.

Johns, J. (1997). *Basic Reading Inventory: Pre-Primer Through Grade Twelve*. Dubuque, IA: Kendall/Hunt.

Lundberg, I., Frost, J., & Peterson, O. P. (1988). Effects of an extensive program for stimulating phonological awareness in preschool children. *Reading Research Quarterly*, 23, 264-284.

Pennsylvania Department of Education. *Reading Instruction Handbook*. Retrieved March 27, 2001, from Pennsylvania Department of Education Web site: http://www.pde.psu.edu/connections/reading/rihand15.htm.

Pinnell, G. S. & Fountas, I. C. (1999). *Matching Books to Readers: Using Leveled Books in Guided Reading, K-3*. Portsmouth, NH: Heinemann.

Pinnell, G. S. Lyons, C. A., Young, P. & Deford, D. E. "The Reading Recovery Program in Ohio," Volume VI (Technical Report). The Ohio State University: Columbus, OH, 1987.

Professional References

Snow, C. E., Burns, M. S., & Griffin, P. (1998). *Preventing Reading Difficulties with Young Children*. Washington, D. C.: National Academy Press.

Stieglitz, E. L. (1997). *The Stieglitz Informal Reading Inventory: Assessing Reading Behaviors from Emergent to Advanced Levels*. Needham Heights, MA: Allyn Bacon.

Tompkins, G. E. (1999). *Teaching Writing: Balancing Process and Product*. New Jersey: Prentice Hall.

Children's Books Cited

Avaricious Aardvarks and Other Alphabet Tongue Twisters by Sandy Sheppard (Standard, 1994).

Can I Keep Him? by Steven Kellogg (Dial Books for Young Readers, 1992).

Hide and Seek by Brown and Carey (Scholastic, Inc., 1994).

More Spaghetti I Say by Rita Golden Gelman (Cartwheel Books, 1993).

Mrs. Wishy-Washy by Joy Cowley (Philomel Books, 1999).

Titch by Pat Hutchins (Aladdin Paperbacks, 1993).

Wagon Wheels by Barbara Brenner (Harper Trophy, 1993).

Whose Mouse Are You? by Robert Kraus (Simon & Schuster, 2000).

Tongue Twister Books

Avaricious Aardvarks and Other Alphabet Tongue Twisters by Sandy Sheppard (Standard, 1994).

Biggest Tongue Twisters Book in the World by Gyles Brandreth (Random House, 1992).

Busy Buzzing Bumblebees and Other Tongue Twisters by Alvin Schwartz (Harper Collins, 1982).

Creepy Crawly Critters and Other Halloween Tongue Twisters by Nola Buck (Harper Collins, 1996).

Santa's Short Suit Shrunk: And Other Christmas Tongue Twisters by Nola Buck (Harper Collins, 1998).

Six Sick Sheep: One Hundred One Tongue Twisters by Joanna Cole and Stephanie Calmenson (Beech Tree Books, 1993).

The World's Greatest Collection of Knock Knock Jokes and Tongue Twisters by Bob Phillips (Barbour, 1995).

World's Toughest Tongue Twisters by Joseph Rosenbloom (Sterling, 1987).

Rhyming Books

A Light in the Attic by Shel Silverstein (Harper Collins, 1981).

Children's Counting-out Rhymes, Fingerplays, Jump Rope and Bounce Ball Chants and Other Rhythms: A Comprehensive English-Language Reference by Gloria Delamar (McFarland, 1983).

The Eentsy, Weentsy Spider: Fingerplays and Action Rhymes by Joanna Cole and Stephanie Calmenson (Mulberry Books, 1991).

Falling Up: Poems and Drawings by Shel Silverstein (Harper Collins, 1996).

Fox in Socks by Dr. Seuss (Random House, 1976).

Hop on Pop by Dr. Suess (Random House, 1976).

I Knew Two Who Said Moo: A Counting and Rhyming Book by Judi Barret and Daniel Moreton (Simon & Schuster, 2000).

Is Your Mama a Llama? by Deborah Guarino (Scholastic, 1989).

Miss Mary Mack: And Other Children's Street Rhymes by Joanna Cole and Stephanie Calmenson (William Morrow & Co., 1990).

One Fish Two Fish Red Fish Blue Fish by Dr. Seuss (Random House, 1976).

Peanut Butter and Jelly: A Play Rhyme by Nadine Bernard Westcott (Viking Penguin, 1991).

Where the Sidewalk Ends: The Poems & Drawing of Shel Silverstein by Shel Silverstein (Harper Collins, 2000).

Web Sites

Tongue Twister Web Sites

http://www.fun-with-words.com

http://www.night.net/christmas/f-twisters1.html (Christmas Tongue Twisters)

http://www.lightsup.com/twister.htm

http://msowww.anu.edu.au/~ralph/tt.html

http://thinks.com/words/tonguetwisters.htm

Web Sites for Leveled Reading

http://registration.beavton.k12.or.us/lbdb/default.htm

http://www.leveled books.com

Additional Professional Resources

Cunningham, P. M., Hall, D. P., & Cunningham, J. W. (2000). *Guided Reading the Four-Blocks® Way*. Greensboro, NC: Carson-Dellosa Publishing.

Cunningham, P. M & Allington, R. L. (1999). *Classrooms That Work: They Can All Read and Write (2nd ed.)*. New York, NY: Longman.

Jordano, K. & Callella-Jones, T. (1998). *Fall Phonemic Awareness Songs and Rhymes.* Huntington Beach, CA: Creative Teaching Press.

Jordano, K. & Callella-Jones, T. (1998). *Spring Phonemic Awareness Songs and Rhymes.* Huntington Beach, CA: Creative Teaching Press.

Jordano, K & Callella-Jones, T. (1998). *Winter Phonemic Awareness Songs and Rhymes.* Huntington Beach, CA: Creative Teaching Press.

Kohfeldt, J. (2000). *Tongue Twisters to Teach Phonemic Awareness and Phonics: Beginning Blends & Digraphs.* Greensboro, NC: Carson-Dellosa Publishing.

Kohfeldt, J. (2000). *Tongue Twisters to Teach Phonemic Awareness and Phonics: Beginning Consonants and Vowels.* Greensboro, NC: Carson-Dellosa Publishing.

Kohfeldt, J., King, A. W., & Collier, H. S. (2000). *Guess the Covered Word for First Grade.* Greensboro, NC: Carson-Dellosa Publishing.

Kohfeldt, J., King, A. W., & Collier, H. S. (2000). *Guess the Covered Word for Second Grade.* Greensboro, NC: Carson-Dellosa Publishing.

Kohfeldt, J., King, A. W., & Collier, H. S. (2000). *Guess the Covered Word for Third Grade.* Greensboro, NC: Carson-Dellosa Publishing.

Kohfeldt, J., King, A. W., & Collier, H. S. (2000). *Guess the Covered Word for Fourth Grade.* Greensboro, NC: Carson-Dellosa Publishing.

Kohfeldt, J., King, A. W., & Collier, H. S. (2000). *Guess the Covered Word for Fifth Grade.* Greensboro, NC: Carson-Dellosa Publishing.

Young, S. D. (1996). *The Scholastic Rhyming Dictionary.* New York: Scholastic, Inc.

